£2.50

The Method and Theory of V. Gordon Childe

Economic, Social and Cultural Interpretations of Prehistory

BARBARA MCNAIRN

Edinburgh
*University
Press*

© Barbara McNairn 1980
EDINBURGH UNIVERSITY PRESS
22 George Square, Edinburgh
ISBN 0 85224 389 8
Printed in Great Britain by
Redwood Burn Limited
Trowbridge & Esher

Contents

Contents

Acknowledgements

I am grateful to Dr Trevor Watkins, Professors
Glyn Daniel, Colin Renfrew and Stuart Piggott for
their help and encouragement in the preparation
of this text. Special thanks to John McNairn for
the many long and stimulating conversations
on all aspects of Childe's work.

Introduction

Since it is now widely known that classification systems and interpretative models play a crucial role in shaping the archaeologist's view of the past, it is evident that the theoretical basis of archaeology needs to be evaluated before a clear understanding of the past can be obtained. To this end it is necessary to build up an historical perspective, for present theory and methodology can only be fully understood when seen as part of a developmental process; we have inherited from past archaeologists not only their accumulated store of data but also their classification systems and interpretative devices.

This work examines the method and theory of V. Gordon Childe (1892–1957), one of the most outstanding and influential figures in the development of the discipline. During his lifetime Childe was best known and especially valued for the depth and breadth of his vision of European and Oriental prehistory. Above all he was seen as 'the systematizer, the lineal descendant of Montelius as an acute and unwearied constructor of chronological schemes, the man who could survey the European scene with scholarly detachment and always distinguish the prehistoric woods amid the close-set trees of archaeological detail' (Piggott 1958a, 77). At a time when the major trend was towards detailed, particularistic research, Childe's texts such as *The Dawn of European Civilization* (1925), *The Danube in Prehistory* (1929), or *Prehistoric Communities of the British Isles* (1940) stand out as great works of synthesis patterning the whole of European prehistory. Childe had succeeded in collating work which had hitherto been scattered throughout Europe in various libraries and museums. The geographical and linguistic barriers separating the individual centres of research were thus broken down and European archaeologists were provided with an overall framework for their enquiries.

As well as his work as a synthesiser, however, Childe made

other important contributions to archaeology. A significant part of his work was concerned with explicitly methodological, theoretical and philosophical issues, work which in many ways anticipated the later developments of the discipline in the sixties and seventies. As early as 1935 Childe was directly stating his aims and methods in archaeology (1935c), and in the forties he was suggesting a role for archaeology in the social sciences (1946d). Throughout his career he was actively involved in interpreting and revising the classification systems then employed in the discipline, i.e. culture and the three ages. This was important to him since he believed that a significant and systematic classification was the first criterion of a scientific discipline (1935c).

Childe was undoubtedly the principal contributor to archaeological methodology in the first half of this century. Of equal importance in the growth of what Clarke (1973) has termed 'critical self consciousness' within the discipline was his work on historical and philosophical theory. Indeed Childe might be said to be the first archaeologist to employ both an explicit methodology and a clearly defined historical and social theory. Although he did not consider the possibility of archaeology generating its own historical laws, he did envisage it as having an important role to play in the construction of such laws. Here he held that archaeology together with anthropology as twin branches of the science of man could provide the basis for the reliable induction of laws on the historical process, the specific role of archaeology being to test the schemes advanced by ethnographers on the basis of their synchronic analyses of contemporary cultures (1946d).

Childe was searching for laws of history which were scientific in basis and in his eyes free from the subjectivity of cultural background. This quest for objectivity led him to examine various types of historical model, for example the religious, the magical, the anthropological and the Marxist. In choosing Marxism as his historical model Childe considered it to be particularly suited to archaeological interpretation.

> Since 'means of production' figure so conspicuously in the archaeological record, I suppose most prehistorians are inclined to be so far Marxists as to wish to assign them a determining role among the behaviour patterns that have fossilised. (1958a, 72)

However, this affinity between Marxist theory and the necessity for the archaeologist to make inferences from the material remains of past societies cannot be seen as the overriding factor influencing his choice. Childe held strong philosophical views on the nature of reality as a self-sufficient and constantly changing process. In his eyes Marxism was the only historical model to approximate to this viewpoint; the others failed on account of their inability to accept change (1945c, 21–6). Childe's interest in epistemology added depth to his thinking especially in the later years when he formalised his thesis. Indeed it is very fortunate that Childe made the philosophical basis of his thought explicit for this affords an excellent opportunity to examine the relationship between a personal philosophy and the work of a distinguished archaeologist.

In 'Retrospect', a brief autobiographical note written shortly before his death in 1957, Childe made it clear that he saw his major contribution to archaeology to be essentially theoretical.

> The most original and useful contributions that I may have made to prehistory are certainly not novel data rescued by brilliant excavation from the soil or by patient research from dusty museum cases, nor yet well founded chronological schemes nor freshly defined cultures, but rather interpretative concepts and methods of explanation.
> (1958a, 69)

During his lifetime, however, his explicitly theoretical work was largely ignored by his contemporaries and even today is not well known. Here an attempt is made to redress the balance, not by depreciating Childe's role as a synthesiser nor by overstating his explicit concern with theory, but rather by viewing both these aspects of his work as integral parts of an overall enquiry into prehistory.

This book has no claims to being an exhaustive study of Childe's life work. Rather it is an examination of what the author considers to be the major methodological, theoretical and philosophical foundations of his thought, together with an analysis of his overall interpretation of European and Near Eastern prehistory.

1

The Synthesis of European and
Near Eastern Prehistory

V. Gordon Childe was born in 1892 in New South Wales,
Australia; his father was the Rev. S. H. Childe. He was edu-
cated at the Church of England Grammar School, Sydney and
at Sydney University where he graduated in Latin, Greek and
Philosophy in 1913. In the following years he studied 'greats'
(Classics and Philosophy) at Oxford where he gained a First
(1917), at the same time completing a B.Litt. course under
Professor John Myres and Sir Arthur Evans on the subject of
Indo-European origins. This research was to have a significant
influence on the subsequent development of Childe's thought,
providing him with the initial motivation to enter the study of
European prehistory.

> Like Gustav Kossinna I came to prehistory from com-
> parative philology; I began the study of European archae-
> ology in the hope of finding the cradle of the Indo-Euro-
> peans and of identifying their primitive culture. Reading
> my Homer and my Veda with the guidance of Schrader
> and Jevons, Zimmer and Wilamowitz-Moellendorf, I was
> thrilled by the discoveries of Evans in Prehellenic Crete
> and of Wace and Thomson in prehistoric Thessaly. Indeed
> I hoped to find archaeological links between the latter area
> and some tract north of the Balkans whence similar links
> might also lead to Iran and India. This search – naturally
> fruitless – was the theme of my B.Litt thesis at Oxford and
> set me trying to discover in the libraries of Oxford and
> London about the already celebrated 'Pre-Mycenean' pot-
> tery of the Ukraine and hence of its analogues in the
> Balkans, Transylvania and Central Europe. (1958a, 69)

Childe, however, did not pursue his research further at this
point but returned to Australia to become actively involved in
what he was later to term 'a sentimental excursion into Australian politics' (1958a, 69). During the remaining two years of
the First World War he participated in the anti-conscription

movement as a member of the Australian Union of Democratic Control. In 1919 he became private secretary to John Storey, who in the following year was appointed premier of New South Wales. Storey's death in 1921, however, effectively put an end to Childe's political career and he returned to England the following year.

It is significant in this context that Childe's first book did not concern archaeology but Australian politics. *How Labour Governs*, published in 1923 by a small left-wing press in London (i.e. the Labour Research Department of the Communist Party), was an analysis of the development of the labour movement in Australia during the first two decades of the twentieth century. *How Labour Governs* has been seen as a gesture of withdrawal from politics. Not only was Childe convinced that the structure of the labour movement made timidity and corruption inevitable, but he was also persuaded of the sentimentality of engaging in politics on behalf of a class in which there was increasing apathy and disunity (Smith 1964, ix). Childe's withdrawal however, was not a withdrawal from the left, but rather from 'the vulgar reactionary quality of much of Australian social and political life' (Gollan 1964, 62).

On his return to England Childe spent several years researching into the problems of European origins, both from an archaeological and philological perspective, visiting continental libraries, museums and sites as an important aspect of his enquiry (Green 1977, 23ff.). The outcome was the publication of two major texts, *The Dawn of European Civilization* (1925) and its less well-known sequel *The Aryans* (1926).

The Dawn was first and foremost an archaeological textbook containing descriptive surveys of a multiplicity of cultures scattered in time and space throughout prehistoric Europe. Many of these cultures, in particular those in south-east Europe, were relatively unknown to British archaeologists at the time, their inclusion in the text being the direct outcome of the author's own travels. As a reference book *The Dawn* thus gave the specialist a secondary source, descriptive of European cultures to circa 1500 B.C. (Piggott 1958a, 75). To the modern reader, however, these long and elaborate descriptions fall short of the standards required by the scientific method. The approach is on the whole highly intuitive, there being no standardised method of describing individual items, classes of items or indeed cultures. Furthermore the text abounds with terms such as 'typical' and 'characteristic' which today would require more precise definition. Neither are the visual aids, which are few and far between, at all helpful, resembling bad artistic impressions rather than scientific illustrations (Piggott 1958a, 77; Crawford 1926, 90).

It was not so much the descriptions of individual cultures which made *The Dawn* such an important text in the development of European prehistory. Written at a time when archaeological research was generally conducted on a regional basis, Childe's synthesis provided European scholars with an overall framework within which their particular researches could be placed. Indeed the pattern of prehistory advanced in *The Dawn* was to become the standard framework for scholars over the next thirty years. Before going on to discuss the main structural elements in this pattern, however, it is essential to consider the overall objective of the text. In the preface Childe summed up his major theme as 'the foundation of European civilization as a peculiar and individual manifestation of the human spirit' (1925a, xiii). Throughout his career he was fascinated by what he saw as the essentially progressive nature of modern European society, believing this to be the end result of a long process stretching back into prehistory. Above all he valued the qualities of 'energy, independence and inventiveness' which in his eyes differentiated the modern European from his Oriental counterpart (1925a, xiii, xiv).

Childe saw his main task in *The Dawn* to trace the origins of the new progressive force leading to modern western civilisation and here he attempted to seek a reconciliation between two rival viewpoints.

> On this topic sharply opposed views are current. One school maintains that Western Civilization only began in historic times after 1000 B.C. in a little corner of the Mediterranean and that its true prehistory is not to be found in Europe but in the Ancient East. On the other hand, some of my colleagues would discover the origin of all the higher elements in human culture in Europe itself. I can subscribe to neither of these extreme views; the truth seems to me to lie in between them. (1925a, xiii)

Childe thus attempted to reach a balanced explanation of the foundations of European culture within the context of two opposing schools of thought; the Orientalists, who held that the cultural development of prehistoric Europe was dependent on the diffusion of Oriental civilisation, and the Occidentalists, who saw the evolution of European prehistory as essentially a self-sufficient process. Although at the time evolution and diffusion were generally considered to be mutually exclusive opposites (Daniel 1971, 75–9), the debate between the two schools did not fall into a neat diffusionist versus evolutionist dichotomy. The situation was complicated by the fact that the major protagonists of both schools were firm diffusionists. On the one hand G. Elliot Smith (1928), the leader of the Oriental school, stressed the unique contribution made to world progress by the Egyptian 'Children of the Sun' whose globe-wandering activities brought civilisation to the whole world. On the other, Gustav Kossinna (1921), the major exponent of the Western school, attributed what he considered all the higher elements in human culture to another wandering people, the Indo-Europeans or the Aryans.

When we come to evaluate Childe's reconciliation between the two schools, it is immediately obvious that he has not in fact effected a compromise between Oriental and Occidental diffusionism, but between Oriental diffusion and the independent evolution of European culture.

> The Occident was, I would submit, indebted to the Orient for the rudiments of the arts and crafts that initiated man's emancipation from bondage to his environment and for the foundation of those spiritual ties that co-ordinate human endeavours. But the peoples of the West were not slavish imitators; they adapted the gifts of the East and united the contributions made by Africa and Asia into a new and organic whole capable of developing along its own original lines. (1925a, xiii)

Childe postulated that there were two main phases in European prehistory after the Palaeolithic; in the first the development of European culture was determined by diffusion from the Orient, and in the second European culture developed along its own independent lines. He argued that the original priority of the Orient over the Occident was due to favourable climatic conditions in the former area.

> The effect of the glaciations of northern Europe must have been to produce in Africa and south-western Asia a moister and more temperate climate than prevails there to-day. While conditions in our Continent only permitted the sort of life still lived by Esquimaux, the contemporary inhabi-

tants of North Africa and Western Asia enjoyed an environment eminently favourable to cultural progress. . .

It must then be admitted that true civilizations had grown up, and were well established in the Ancient East while Europe was still sunk in epipalaeolithic barbarism. The well-known identity between the earliest domestic animals and cultivated plants of Europe and Asia is therefore a valid argument for the view that the gifts that distinguish neolithic culture from the palaeolithic, came to Europe from the Ancient East. (1925a, 22, 23)

Childe considered that the turning point in Europe's relationship with the Orient lay in the Bronze Age.

By the sixteenth century B.C. the new organism was already functioning and the point had arrived when the Westerners were ready to assume the rôle of masters. Among the Early Bronze Age peoples of the Aegean, the Danube Valley, Scandinavia and Britain, we can recognise already the expression of those very qualities of energy, independence and inventiveness which distinguish the western world from Egypt, India or China. (1925a, xiii, xiv)

From the Bronze Age onwards he seemed assured of the subsequent development of European culture into modern civilisation and for that reason he terminated *The Dawn* at this point.

My task is then to exhibit the creation out of the cultural capital common to many lands of the new force, the growth of which has ultimately transformed the face of the world. Since the germs of the new are evidently active in the Middle Bronze Age that period puts a natural term to the enquiry.(1925a, xiv)

Since *The Dawn* was specifically concerned with the first phase in European prehistory, the main argument in the text is firmly Orientalist and diffusionist. Thus if viewed out of context, it could quite easily give a false impression of his overall intellectual position at this time.

The debate between the Orientalists and the Occidentalists was largely perpetuated by the absence of an absolute chronology for prehistoric Europe. At the time, the only method of estimating the dates of the culture sequences, established in Europe by stratigraphical and typological techniques was to tie them in with the historically dated systems of the Near Eastern civilisations. This was impossible, however, without making two important diffusionist assumptions. Firstly one had to assume that cultural similarities existing between Europe and the Near East were the result of 'contact' between the two areas. Secondly one had to assume the direction of the contact (Renfrew 1973, 28–47).

In the first edition of *The Dawn* Childe defined two major channels of diffusion between the Orient and Europe, the Mediterranean Seaway and the Danube Valley. At this time his main emphasis was on the link between the East Mediterranean and the Iberian peninsula. This was a major bone of contention between the Occidental and Oriental schools. While the former saw the development of Iberian culture wholly in insular terms, the latter sought an explanation for important turning-points in this development by reference to Oriental influence.

One of the main issues in the debate concerned the origin of megalithic architecture on the peninsula (1925a, 129–37). At the time, this was an important question not only for the internal development of Iberian culture but for the prehistory of Europe as a whole, since the extensive distribution of mega-lithic architecture was generally considered to be the result of diffusion from a single centre. Where the two schools disagreed was on the question of the location of this presumed centre. While the Occidentalists proposed an Iberian origin, the Orientalists favoured an Egyptian one. The former argued that the dolmen was the local invention of the Mesolithic inhabi-tants of Spain, being in effect an artificial cave and thus an extension of Palaeolithic and Mesolithic burial practices. The latter, however, sought the prototype of the megalith in the Egyptian mastaba, seeing here a rational explanation of many of the features of megalithic sepulchres. In this context they attributed the wide distribution of megaliths to the religious practices of Egyptian prospectors in search of gold.

For Childe there were serious difficulties in both arguments. He did not like the fact that the Orientalists had to change Montelius's classic typological series of megalithic monuments. Instead of postulating a simple linear development from dol-men through passage and gallery graves to megalithic cist, the latter viewed both the dolmen and megalithic cist as degenerate forms (1925aa, 131). Secondly he was not altogether happy with the prospector hypothesis since no valuable metal had in fact been discovered in megalithic tombs. But he was even less convinced by the Occidental argument. While he was fairly sympathetic to the idea of some continuity between Palaeolithic and Neolithic burial practices, he was unwilling to derive Aegean and Egyptian burial practices from the West. 'It would be absurd to argue that the western barbarians taught the Egyptians and Cretans the cult of the dead' (1925a, 133).

Here Childe attempted to balance the two viewpoints. While he accepted the Oriental initiative he was not unappreciative of the Occidental contribution. At first he envisaged the initial diffusion of the idea of the dolmen.

> Perhaps early voyagers did in fact originally introduce the idea of the dolmen to the West. But their conceptions of the future life were not wholly strange to those of the aborigines. The latter then may have adopted the new idea together with some arts such as the polishing of stone and navigation and have spread it in a barbarized version throughout the western world. (1925a, 133, 134)

At a later date, however, he postulated the arrival of actual colonists, 'traders' rather than 'prospectors' from the eastern Mediterranean bringing with them the corbelled vault and metallurgy. 'Thus there arose in the Iberian peninsula a veritable counterpart of the maritime civilization of the Aegean, albeit infused with original elements' (1925a, 137).

Childe did not, however, consider that these megalithic builders had made any significant contribution to further progress in Europe.

> The great civilization of Los Millares in Spain like that of the Arabs later on, succumbed to a process of slow degradation. Perhaps it was too oriental to survive on Western soil. The megalithic-builders of the Atlantic, despite their stupendous monuments, played on the actual evidence derived from the monuments themselves, a much smaller role than recent writers have assigned to them.
> (1925a, 302)

In the second edition of *The Dawn* (1927) they were thus relegated to a position of secondary import and the major emphasis shifted from the Aegean–Iberian seaway to the 'Danubian thoroughfare'. Childe held the culture of the Danubian peasants to be one of the most progressive in European prehistory. In his own words the Danubians 'created a civilization whence pulsed the life-blood of progress throughout the greater part of our continent' (1925a, 171).

The origin of the Danubian culture was again another important point of controversy between the Oriental and Occidental schools (1925a, 175). Schliz had ascribed the Danubian culture to the immigration of Cro-Magnons from the West, Kossinna to the descendants of the Ertebolle folk from north-west Germany. Vassits on the other hand looked to Troy. Childe, while not specifying direct immigration from Troy, did support a Mediterranean origin.

> In a general way the Danubian culture has Mediterranean affinities. The *Spondylus* shells point in that direction; figurines are common in the Mediterranean basin; the spiral though at home in the Danube, subsequently flourished in the Aegean; the occurrence of shoe-last celts in Thessaly I may be significant. The scanty anthropometric data could be interpreted as supporting a Mediterranean origin. A skull from the lowest stratum at Vinča was long headed. Schliz' study of the skeletons found with spiral-meander pottery in Silesia, Bohemia, Saxony and in the Rhine valley revealed a short, moderately dolichocephalic race. He even admits a certain resemblance in the skulls to Sergi's Mediterraneans, but declares there are important differences and ultimately claims the Danubians for a branch of the Nordic race. Finally the grains from Danubian II settlements (none certainly belonging to the first period have been studied) belong to species which are common in the Mediterranean basin. (1925a, 176)

Whereas Childe saw the civilising influence of the sea-voyagers ending in stagnation, he considered the Danubians to have made important contributions to European progress. In outlining the reasons for this he was careful to balance the Oriental and Occidental elements in the creation of the new European cultures. At the same time he referred to the incursion of nomads into the Danubian province, considering these to have prevented cultural stagnation in the north and to have introduced bronze metallurgy into Hungary.

> The cultural province whose fortunes have just been sketched turns out to be the pivot of early civilization in continental Europe. The Danubian I peasants in their gradual expansion carried with them the domestic animals and cultivated plants and diffused the 'neolithic arts' among their western neighbours. The incursion of nomads

prevented stagnation in the north and introduced the Hungarians to the metal tools and weapons invented long before by the Sumerians. Then the beaker folk linked the Danube commercially with the Aegean and Trojan metallurgy discovered the tin of Bohemia. Out of these impulses arose the Aunjetitz culture upon which both the Nordic and Hungarian bronze ages are based. Finally the Danubians in the Hungarian plain inspired by Bohemian and Mycenean models created out of their own copper culture a Central European civilization that could vindicate its independence of the Mediterranean by force of arms. (1925a, 200–1)

In *The Dawn* Childe argued that the nomads who invaded the Danubian province were derived from a vast complex of Battle-axe cultures spreading from south-east Russia to north-west Germany. And here he represented them as vehicles for Mesopotamian influence reaching the Danubian province via the great European plain.

Aside from this brief outline however, Childe was not concerned to explain in depth why the Danubian cultures should have progressed while their Iberian counterparts declined. At this time he believed that the problem of progress in Europe could only be solved by an interdisciplinary approach; i.e. by archaeology working together with philology. Consequently he deferred a full consideration of the problem until *The Aryans* (1926) in which he examined the philological and archaeological data in some detail.

By the nineteen-twenties, however, the Aryan question was no longer a purely philological one but had acquired a strong racialist component. The original Aryan was popularly depicted as a tall dolichocephalic man with fair hair and blue eyes. Moreover this grouping was widely acclaimed as the highest and most noble of all the human races. The doctrine of the superiority of the Aryan race had a profound effect on all western thought in the early decades of the twentieth century (Snyder 1939, 1962; Poliakov 1974). It was best received however, in Germany where it was popularised through the works of such writers as Arthur de Gobineau and Houston Chamberlain. Here it was to become one of the theoretical foundations of Hitlerism.

History has shown with terrible clarity that each time Aryan blood has become mixed with inferior peoples the

result has been the end of the culture sustaining race. . . .
All that we admire on this earth – science, art, technical
skills and invention – is the creative product of only a small
number of nations, and originally, perhaps of one single
race. All this culture depends on them for its very existence. If these nations are ruined they carry with them all
the beauty of this earth into the grave. . . .

All great cultures of the past have gone on to destruction because the original creative race died of blood
poisoning. Always it has been the same thing – the final
cause for such destruction came from the error that all
culture is independent of man, when just the opposite is
true – creative man must guard his own culture.

This point of view is bound up with the iron law of
necessity and the law of victory for the best and the strong-
est. Who wants to live also must fight, and he who does not
want to fight in this world does not deserve to live. . . . The
man who knows the laws of race and pays no attention to
them . . . hinders the triumph of the best races as well as all
human progress. He joins the sphere . . . of helpless
beasts . . . .

If mankind were to be divided into three categories,
founders, maintainers and destroyers of culture, the
Aryan stock alone would represent the first category of
founders. From them come the fundamentals of all human
creative effort. (Hitler in Snyder 1962, 155–7)

Childe was aware of these developments and warned of the
dangers of the misapplication of the Aryan thesis in modern
politics.

The apotheosis of the Nordics has become linked with
policies of imperialism and world domination: the word
'Ayran' has become the watchword of dangerous factions
and especially of the more brutal and blatant forms of
anti-Semitism. Indeed the neglect and discredit into which
the study of Indo-European philology has fallen in
England are very largely attributable to a legitimate reaction against the extravagancies of Houston Stewart
Chamberlain, and his ilk, and the gravest objection to the
word Aryan is its association with pogroms. (1926a, 164)

The Aryans was largely devoted to tracing the first appearance of the Indo-Europeans in history and to reviewing the
various hypotheses concerning their original homeland. Here

Childe enlisted the aid of linguistic palaeontology, which attempts to reconstruct the original form of the mother tongue from a comparison of known words among the Indo-European languages. This in turn provides an opportunity to reconstruct the original environment of the first Indo-European speakers. The method of linguistic palaeontology is however beset with problems, one of the biggest being the chronological co-ordination of one trait with another. Furthermore the general distribution of these constructed traits has proven to be so wide as to accommodate several conflcting theories (Mallory 1976).

After reviewing the arguments for an Asiatic, central European, north European and south Russian homeland, Childe tentatively identified the latter as the most probable centre of origin for the first Indo-Europeans (1926a, 183–204). Like Kossinna, whom he considered his chief opponent in the field, Childe equated the vast complex of Battle-axe cultures, spreading from north-west Germany across eastern and central Europe to the south Russian steppes, with the original Indo-Europeans. Childe, however, vehemently opposed his opponent's thesis of a north-west European homeland for the authors of the Battle-axe cultures and argued instead for the priority of the south Russian area. While Kossinna envisaged diffusion from the Jutland region throughout Europe and into south Russia and beyond by bands of warrior pastoralists and cultivators, Childe reversed the direction of these invasions, seeing the Jutland culture as the result of migration from the south-east.

Interestingly, both viewpoints relied to a large extent upon archaeological data since the clues afforded by linguistic palaeontology were either so general that they accommodated both centres without much difficulty, or they were so hypothetical that they could be easily ignored if unsuitable. The German school in particular was so convinced of the validity of the archaeological case for a northern origin that they tended to make minimal use of linguistic data. Basically their main argument was that the Nordic Battle-axe culture could be satisfactorily explained as the result of an indigenous evolutionary process in north-west Germany (1926a, 164–8). After the recession of the ice-cap at the end of the last glaciation circa 10000 B.C. the area of the Baltic depression became occupied by descendants of palaeolithic reindeer hunters. On the shores of the numerous lakes throughout the region these hunters created a vigorous hunting-fishing economy with highly developed bone and flint industries (Maglemosian). Kossinna regarded these as the ancestors of both the Indo-Europeans and the Finns, supposing that they spoke an agglutinative tongue from which Indo-European and Finno-Ugrian later evolved. About 6000 B.C. the climate in Europe became warmer, resulting in the further retreat of the ice-cap and the subsequent filling up of the Baltic depression by salt water. While the more conservative of the hunter-fishers (the Finns) spread to the north and east in order to retain a lifestyle based on a fresh water economy, the more adaptable took advantage of the new environmental conditions and created the famous Ertebolle culture. About 4500 B.C. these people went on to domesticate plants and animals, and to invent pottery and polished stone axes. Kossinna then envisaged a southward migration which was to account for the basic division of the Indo-European group into 'satem' and 'centum' languages. Those who were to pronounce 'k' as 's' went south and created the Danubian civilisation. In Hungary they discovered and began to exploit local copper ores, casting their distinctive battle-axes. Meanwhile the section left on the Baltic learned the art of dolmen building which had been transmitted to Scandinavia via Ireland from Spain. Then there began a phase of rapid development in the arts and of further expansion in all directions. Although Kossinna's main argument relied heavily on archaeological data, it should be noted that he also attempted to draw anthropological support for his thesis. At a time when race and language were seen as equated, this was standard practice. Kossinna thus sought in the prehistoric remains of ancient Germany for tall dolichocephalic skeletons, the fore-runners of the modern Nordic type.

Childe challenged both the anthropological and archaeological evidence for Kossinna's thesis. Firstly, he argued that the skeletal evidence from northern Germany was not securely dated, nor did it reveal a pure dolichocephalic type.

> In the sphere of ethnology, the bases of the theory are not so stable as might be wished. The skulls on which Kossinna relies to prove the Nordic character of his Maglemose-Dobbertin folk are by no means certainly dated; in any case the Nordic race can scarcely be derived from the western Cro-Magnon stock, but had eastern or Central European antecedents. It can nevertheless be regarded as

generally probable that a sort of proto-Nordic element was present in the North in the days of the Maglemose culture and of the later kitchen-middens, as it had been in the last phase of the Old Stone Age in South Germany. On the other hand the bodies interred in the early dolmens, as Kossinna himself points out, belonged according to Kan Fürst to individuals who, although dolichocephalic, were short of stature, i.e. to members of that same Eurafrican race which built the other dolmens in Western Europe and the long barrows in Britain. (1926a, 179)

In common with the majority of his contemporaries Childe agreed that the original Aryans belonged to the Nordic race as characterised in northern Europe today (1926a, 159–64). In addition, he argued that there were important elements in the culture of north-west Germany which could not be explained as the results of internal development, but on the contrary could only be regarded as intrusive. In particular he was referring to the battle-axe which both he and Kossinna saw as the characteristic symbol of Aryan culture. In contrast to the simplicity of Kossinna's thesis of internal development from palaeolithic antler horns, Childe's argument for a south Russian origin for the battle-axe is long and tortuous involving a number of unsubstantiated assumptions.

Childe maintained that the German stone battle-axes were in fact imitations of the copper axe-adze of which there were frequent examples in Hungary. These in turn he explained by assuming that they were amalgamations of two Mesopotamian axes, one with the blade parallel to the shaft and the other with the blade at right angles to the shaft. On this basis he inferred that the development of the axe-adze could be most satisfactorily explained as occurring in the South Russian steppes since this area had possible contacts with Mesopotamia in the third millennium. As he himself admitted, however, this hypothetical typological series could not be used as proof until validated in the archaeological record (1926a, 190).

In *The Aryans*, as in *The Dawn*, Childe was ultimately searching for an explanation of the foundations of modern western civilisation. Now, however, since the data had been extended to include philological as well as archaeological sources, the overall argument is much more comprehensive than was previously attempted. Basically, Childe emphasised that man's social evolution is closely related to his intellectual development which is in turn influenced by his language.

> Man's progress from savagery to civilization is intimately bound up with the advance of abstract thinking, which enables him to rise above the chaos of particular sensations and fashion therefrom an ordered cosmos. The growth of reasoning in its turn goes hand in hand with the development of language . . . . Words are the very stuff of thought . . . . Moreover, intellectual progress may to a large extent be measured by the refinement of language. (1926a, 3)

Consequently as indicated previously he did not consider that the problem of progress in Europe could be tackled by archaeology alone, but by archaeology working in conjunction with philology.

> Favourable climatic conditions, peculiar natural resources, a happy conjuncture of trade routes do not suffice to explain this phenomenon; behind it lurks the true historic fact of personal initiative. That archaeology cannot grasp, indeed the concrete person lies beyond the sphere of prehistory. But an approximation thereto in terms of racial individuality is attainable with the aid of philology. Language, albeit an abstraction, is yet a more subtle and pervasive criterion of individuality than the culture-group formed by comparing flints and potsherds or the 'races' of the skull-measurer. And it is precisely in Europe, where the critical point of cultural evolution lies enshrouded in the gloom of the prehistoric period, that the linguistic principles just enunciated are most readily applicable. . . . It is perhaps then not overbold to hope that a collaboration between the two prehistoric disciplines of philology and archaeology, at least in this modest domain, may help to solve certain problems that either science alone is powerless to resolve. (1926a, 4–5)

The main argument in the text, however, is clearly a philological one, the role of archaeology being to supplement and clarify individual points. For Childe the clue to progress in Europe lay in the Indo-European languages spoken by our ancestors. Not only did he consider these languages to be particularly fine vehicles of thought, but he also emphasised that they reflected the high intellectual development of the Indo-Europeans.

The Indo-European languages and their assumed parent-speech have been throughout exceptionally delicate and flexible instruments of thought. They were almost unique, for instance, in possessing a substantive verb and at least a rudimentary machinery for building subordinate clauses that might express conceptual relations in a chain of ratiocination. It follows then that the Aryans must have been gifted with exceptional mental endowments, if not in enjoyment of a high material culture. This is more than mere inference. It is no accident that the first great advances towards abstract natural science were made by the Aryan Greeks and the Hindus, not by the Babylonians or the Egyptians, despite their great material resources and their surprising progress in *techniques* – in astronomical observation for example. In the moralization of religion too Aryans have played a prominent rôle. The first great world religions which addressed their appeal to all men irrespective of race or nationality, Buddhism and Zoroastrianism, were the works of Aryans, propagated in Aryan speech. . . . Nor were the potentialities of Aryan speech solely intellectual. Poetry in which a fixed metrical structure combines with sweet sounding words to embody beautiful ideas seems peculiarly Aryan. (1926a, 4, 5)

In assessing what he saw as the positive contribution of the Aryans to world progress, Childe considered that it was in continental Europe where their role as 'founders of Western Civilization' was most evident (1926a, 209, 210). Here, as in *The Dawn* he contrasted their achievement with that of the megalithic builders where he saw 'not a vestige of progress' (1926a, 210)

It seems as if these people were wholly absorbed in the cult of the dead and as if superstitious observances monopolized and paralysed all their activities. Complete stagnation ruled in industry, and to find parallels to their culture we have only to visit the Pacific Islands which may have been exposed to a similar influence. (1926a, 210)

In Britain he traced the first signs of progress to the Battle-axe invaders whom he saw as Aryan.

The rich and varied furniture of the intruders' round barrows is in striking contrast to the monotonous poverty of the grave goods from the older long barrows. We know now that the battle-axe wielders were admixed with Aryans, and the truly Western civilization which hence-

18

forth ruled in Britain was obviously promoted by them.
(1926a, 210)

Again in Scandinavia, he attributed the rise of a creative and
original culture primarily to Aryan influence.

In Scandinavia the contrast to France and the Iberian
peninsula is even more fundamental. Here, too, men built
megalithic graves, but their furniture here is totally different to anything discoverable further west. And besides the
megalithic tombs were other graves covering the remains
of a people, who, whether they came from South Russia or
represented a section of the pre-dolmenic population,
were, we believe, Aryan in character. It was these who
inspired the higher developments even in the megalithic
culture of the North. The interaction of the two types of
civilization was the mainspring of a rapid progress. And
ultimately the division was overcome; the Aryans imposed their authority and their culture – partly, if you will,
a borrowed culture – on the whole region, welded the
disparate racial groups and the scattered clans into a
national unity in which western and eastern ideas were
blended to an European whole and called forth a progressive society no less brilliant in trade than in war. The gulf
between French and Scandinavian culture at the beginning of the IInd millenium is enormous. The superiority of
the former is the measure of the contribution made by the
Aryan element to European civilization. (1926a, 210, 211)

In the Danubian province, while he did not associate the
initial appearance of the Aryans with an immediate rise in the
standard of culture, he did nevertheless argue that the subsequent development of a highly original culture was primarily
due to their influence.

Just where the Nordic invasions had been most persistent
we find a Bronze Age art and industry which are truly
European in their originality. The ferment which trans-
muted the societies of agricultural clans into the heroic
tribes of the Bronze and Iron Ages, thus opening the way
to initiative and individuality, we regard as Aryan.

Thus the Aryans do appear everywhere as promoters of
true progress and in Europe their expansion marks the
moment when the prehistory of our continent begins to
diverge from that of Africa or the Pacific. (1926a, 211)

In *The Dawn* Childe had distinguished within the European

Bronze Age the 'germs' of the new 'force' which was, in his eyes, to culminate in modern civilisation. While he had attributed this to a fusion of Occidental and Oriental culture in which Battle-axe invaders from South Russia played a significant role, he had not been fully explicit as regards the nature of this role. In *The Aryans* however, the reasons for their importance became clear. It is not only because they were the vehicles of Mesopotamian influence, but also because they possessed a highly flexible and delicate linguistic structure, which, according to Childe, was a necessary prerequisite of progress.

Childe was careful to point out that his was not a racialist explanation of progress but a philological one.

> How precisely did the Aryans achieve all this? It was not through the superiority of their material culture. We have rejected the idea that a peculiar genius resided in the conformation of Nordic skulls. We do so with all the more confidence that, by the time Aryan genius found its true expression in Greece and Rome, the pure Nordic strain had been for the most absorbed in the Mediterranean substratum: the lasting gift bequeathed by Aryans to the conquered peoples was neither a higher material culture nor a superior physique, but . . . a more excellent language and the mentality it generated. (1926a, 211, 212)

At the same time, however, he did not consider the assumed physical characteristics of the original Aryans to be entirely irrelevant.

> The fact that the first Aryans were Nordics was not without importance. The physical qualities of that stock did enable them by the bare fact of superior strength to conquer even more advanced peoples and so to impose their language on areas from which their bodily type has almost completely vanished. This is the truth underlying the panegyrics of the Germanists: the Nordics' superiority in physique fitted them to be the vehicles of a superior language. (1926a, 212)

In his later work, Childe was to make no reference to this early explanation of progress in Bronze Age Europe. Indeed during the thirties and forties, because he chose to deny the progressive quality of European prehistory, he effectively shelved the problem.

In 'Retrospect' he attributed the strengthening of his Orientalist position not so much to the inherent merits of the Orientalist stance, but to his revulsion from an Occidentalist thesis which he saw as providing ideological support for Nazism (1958a, 72). While he does not comment on his position as regards the Aryan question at this time, it is clear from his writings during the thirties and forties that he was bitterly opposed to the use of the Aryan thesis to validate the persecution of 'non-Aryan races'.

It was not until the mid-fifties that Childe again began to appreciate the creative quality of the European Bronze Age. By this time, however, he attempted to explain this phenomenon purely in terms of sociological and historical inferences made from the archaeological record and without reference to the role of the notorious Aryans. This development will be discussed later in the chapter. First, it is necessary to look at his work on the Oriental sequences if a full appreciation of his synthesis is to be gained.

During the first two decades of the twentieth century, what Childe regarded as the first scientific excavations in the Orient were just beginning, and their results known only from brief reports in the *Antiquaries Journal, The Journal of the Royal Asiatic Society* or *The Illustrated London News* (1958a, 71). In particular, the excavation of the forgotten Indus civilisation, the sensational discoveries in the Royal tombs at Ur and the excavation of the neolithic settlements at Badari had greatly extended the nineteenth-century picture of the ancient East.

Childe's basic contribution in this context was to incorporate the fresh data into an overall scheme of the development of Oriental civilisation. In *The Most Ancient East*, published in 1928, he presented a survey of the rise of civilisation in Egypt, Mesopotamia and India, from the earliest farmers until circa 3000 B.C.

In Egypt his account begins with a description of the finds from El Badari, newly excavated by Guy Brunton and Caton-Thompson. At the time this was considered to be the earliest neolithic culture yet discovered. Thereafter followed a description of the first and second Predynastic cultures and finally an account of the rise of the dynasts. In Mesopotamia the material was discussed under three major headings; the First Prediluvian Culture, the Second Prediluvian Civilisation and the Sumerian Civilisation at the end of the ivth Millennium, each heading being indicative of a different cultural stage. In India, however, it was not yet possible to trace the development of the Indus civilisation and he could thus only generalise on the mature stage.

In each of the three major centres surveyed, Childe was interested in: (1) presenting a broad description of the geographical context of the culture concerned, (2) indicating the general socio-economic level attained by the culture, (3) outlining the main archaeological types, i.e. bone, ceramics, ivory, flint, etc., and (4) attempting to elucidate the origin of the culture.

These accounts, like their counterparts in *The Dawn*, were largely intuitive and followed no set pattern of approach. Each of the four main areas indicated above were thus not discussed in any particular order, the question of origins for example might occupy the first or last (or indeed both) positions in any one account; important inferences concerning the economy, sociology or ideology were frequently juxtaposed between detailed descriptions of particular items.

In the first edition of *The Most Ancient East*, Childe reserved the final chapter for a consideration of the relationship between the Orient and Europe. Only sixteen pages long, this is perhaps the most significant section in the book in terms of the overall development of his thought. Not only does it contain the essence of his argument in favour of the priority of Oriental invention but it also includes the germs of much of his subsequent work on food production and metallurgy. Childe opened the chapter with an affirmation of the antiquity of Oriental civilisation. Fairly rapidly however, this develops into an assertion of the Orient's priority over European culture.

In the preceding pages I have tried to conjure up a picture of the Oriental world prior to 3000 B.C. The first salient feature in that picture is the hoary antiquity of civilization in the region under review. By the end of the IVth millennium the material culture of Abydos, Ur or Mohenjo Daro would stand comparison with that of Periclean Athens, or of any medieval town. Metallurgy, rightly taken by historians as marking an epoch in human progress, had certainly been practised intelligibly even a thousand years earlier. In no part of Europe outside Crete was metal demonstrably in use before the third millennium, and its general employment on a scale comparable to that exemplified in Susa I dates only from the second.

The stage of higher barbarism represented at Badari and in the Fayum must, on the most modest reckoning, have been reached in the sixth millennium before our era. In the whole of Europe we can attribute to such remote antiquity not a single food-producing community outside Crete, unless perhaps the disgusting savages who left the shell-mounds on the shore of the Littorina Sea cultivated a little barley. . . .

The Orient's claim to the origination of all the primary inventions is thus beyond dispute, once the diffusionist postulate be accepted. (1928, 220, 221)

From this point, Childe went on to attempt to prove the validity of the diffusionist hypothesis by reference to the continuity in the cultural tradition of the Orient, and between the Orient and Europe.

But the accuracy of the postulate is guaranteed by the fundamental continuity that characterised the Oriental world no less than its antiquity. And the same threads that held together the various centres of Oriental civilization can be shown to bind thereto the European barbarisms of prehistory.

This continuity is not just an abstract identity. The foundations of life are not just agriculture and stock raising but the cultivation of cereals and the breeding of cattle, sheep and swine. . . .

Archaeology affords positive proof of the continuity of tradition in metallurgy. In ancient mines in Sinai, the Caucusus, the Austrian Alps, Spain and Cornwall, the hammers used for breaking the ore all consist of a grooved stone, lashed into the fork of a stick by thongs, fitting in the groove. The generic similarity of the oldest tools and weapons is still better known. (1928, 221, 225)

Childe's attempt to confirm his Orientalist stance without any explicit reference to the problem of chronology, however, was not wholly successful. Without an absolute time-scale for prehistoric Europe, neither the priority of oriental invention nor the diffusionist postulate can be fully accepted. This is clear enough in the former case which is obviously a chronological question involving a comparison in time, but it is also true as concerns the latter. Before cultural similarities can be accepted as proof of diffusion they need to be chronologically tested in order to show a continuity in time as well as in space.

Childe never seriously considered the possibility of the independent evolution of European culture before the Bronze Age, and his application of the diffusionist paradigm to this stage in prehistory is evident throughout. It is perhaps most apparent in his search for primary centres of innovation – standard diffusionist practice based on the assumption that all major inventions occurred only once and from thence spread to the rest of the world. Childe insisted, for example, that a primary centre of food production was 'more than just a methodological postulate' (1928, 228) even although at the time he could not support this claim from the archaeological record. He continues,

> It would at least be absurd to suggest that men began cultivating plants whose range in nature is quite limited like wheat and barley, at several independent centres in that circumscribed region. It would be hardly less fantastic to assume that domestication of cattle, sheep and swine happened more than once. The common traits of what is not very happily termed the 'neolithic culture' are too numerous to deny some unity behind it. (1928, 228)

In *The Most Ancient East* Childe advanced several reasons for the diffusion of agriculture from the Orient, all of which he was to uphold throughout his entire career. First, he argued that the primitive methods of agriculture would inevitably lead to soil exhaustion and the necessary migration of the community in search of new land. Secondly, he saw smaller communities breaking off from the mother community because of internal disagreement and, thirdly, he envisaged the conversion of food gatherers into food producers during lean years.

At the same time, he also outlined his argument for the diffusion of civilisation. Basically he saw this as a necessary function of the Orient's demand for raw materials, in particular for the bronze industry, arguing that this led not only to cultural stimulation in supply areas but also to the migration of craftsmen. In the following years Childe was to go into the economic and sociological implications of metallurgy in more depth and this in turn was to result in a more detailed analysis of the mechanisms of diffusion involved in the spread of civilisation.

The first step came with the publication of *The Bronze Age* in 1930, a work which like *The Dawn* was an archaeological synthesis of a period in European prehistory. However, the field covered is much narrower, being confined to the Bronze Age in western Europe and in central Europe north of the Alps. Also the format is quite different; in addition to general summaries of cultural groupings, the text contains large descriptive chapters devoted specifically to Bronze Age typology.

In the first chapter, which contained the major theoretical discussion, Childe introduced two important points referring to the economic and sociological implications of metallurgy. First he argued that the effective working of the metallurgical process involved industrial specialization and thus the freeing of certain members of the community from active involvement in the food quest. Secondly, on the assumption that bronze was the first indispensable article of trade (in contrast to luxury goods) he argued that bronze working required the loss of neolithic self-sufficiency.

This work heralds a significant change in Childe's attitude towards European prehistory. Whereas previously he had stressed the positive aspects of the recipient cultures in contributing to the development of European prehistory, now he paints a very negative picture.

> In our period it is not possible to point to a single vital contribution to material culture originating in Europe outside the Aegean area.
>
> And, if it be argued that this poverty in material culture was counter-balanced by an inherent spiritual superiority, we can point to the cannibal feasts of the Knovíz peoples and the human sacrifices depicted on the Kivik tombstone. Certainly Bronze Age burials suggest a monogamous family and a high status for women. But, after all, few Orientals could actually afford a harem, and the queens of Egypt were buried with sufficient pomp. It would be just silly to say that Scandinavian decorative art was superior to Babylonian or Minoan. And no-one in their senses will compare the Swedish rock-carvings with even a poor Egyptian bas relief of the Trondholm horse with a Sumerian bull of circa 3000 B.C. (1930a, 238–9)

Nevertheless he still assumed a direct cultural link between Bronze Age and modern Europe. However whereas previously he had taken the nature of this link to be self evident, now he is more specific as to its form.

> The roots of modern civilization were struck down deep into this unpromising soil. The general economic and

social structure that may be inferred from the late Bronze Age remains persisted with surprisingly superficial modifications throughout the Roman Period in many parts of the Empire. The native houses and fields of the Roman Britain did not differ essentially from those of the latest Bronze Age. And after all the direct ancestors of the Romans themselves prior to the rule of the Etruscan kinds had been just an Urnfield folk comparable to the inhabitants of the Lausitz and Alpine slopes. Even in the British Isles many elements of pure Bronze Age culture survived unchanged by subsequent migrations and invasions till late in last century. For example, travellers describe huts and a foot-plough, exactly like these known directly or inferred in Bronze Age Britain, as still current in the Hebrides. Despite the upheavals of the Early Iron Age and the Migration Period one is inclined to believe in a considerable continuity both in blood and tradition between the Bronze Age and the modern populations. (1930a, 239)

With his new analysis of bronze working Childe felt himself to be committed to an economic interpretation of archaeological data (1958a, 71). During the thirties and forties he was to explore and define the potential of this approach to the past. The next step came with the rewriting of *The Most Ancient East* in 1934, which was necessitated by the greatly increasing rate of discovery in this field.

Obliged by unexpected new discoveries to rewrite *The Most Ancient East*, I not only read excavation reports but visited Mesopotamia and India. I saw how the beginnings of literacy in three great river valleys coincided with the erection of the first monumental tombs and temples and the aggregation of the population into regular cities. Indeed at Ur and Erech I saw how rustic villages had grown into vast townships just as English villages had grown into manufacturing towns. Now the latter transfiguration was familiarly attributed to an 'industrial revolution'. Demographically the birth of literacy in the Ancient East also corresponded to a revolution, the Urban Revolution. The upward kink in the population graph, deduced from the monuments, must be due at least party to the emergence in addition to the farmers, of a new order of professionals who did not grow or catch their own food. . . . But if the Urban Revolution had added an order of professionals to the farmers, the latter were themselves offspring of a revolution. The adoption of food-production must have been, and from the available data, had been, followed by a still greater expansion of population than on the foregoing analogy would amply justify the term 'Neolithic Revolution'. So in *New Light on the Most Ancient East* (1934), despite the occasional invocation of undocumented events in the wings, a truly historical pageant of economic development was presented on the stage. (1958a, 71)

In the final chapter, now entitled 'The Mechanism of Diffusion', Childe integrated his new economic interpretation of the urban revolution with his Orientalist hypothesis. Here he argued that the economic and sociological processes or urbanism accelerated the diffusion of civilisation from the Orient to Europe. In particular he was referring to three main processes, population increase, trade and war.

As in the Industrial Revolution of Britain the new means of livelihood thus made available would result in a multiplication of the proletariat. At such times population is likely to outgrow the demand for labour and to resort to emigration. The expansion alone would accelerate the processes of diffusion.

Much more profoundly would the new demand for raw materials affect the pace and the very mechanisms of diffusion. Egypt, Sumer, and the Indus cities were now clamouring for vast supplies of timber, building stones and ore, for spices and precious stones for the adornment and service of temples, tombs and public buildings, and for the equipment of artisans and soldiers. The new industrial cities must enter into closer relations with the world of peasant communities that had been created by the first revolution. (1934, 284–5)

Childe argued that these relations were not always friendly, and peaceful trade was often followed by military aggression. This in turn provoked migration and the diffusion of civilisation from the East to the West. In this context he described the origin of Minoan civilisation to refugees fleeing from Menes' conquest at the time of the unification of the Egyptian kingdom.

It was not until 1936, in *Man Makes Himself*, that Childe gave the first full account of his new economic ideas, and here he emphasised his debt to Marxism.

> Marx insisted on the prime importance of economic con-
> ditions, of the social forces of production, and of the
> applications of science as factors in historical change. His
> realist conception of history is gaining acceptance in aca-
> demic circles remote from the party passions inflamed by
> other aspects of Marxism. To the general public and to
> scholars alike, history is tending to become cultural his-
> tory, greatly to the annoyance of Fascists like Dr Frick.
>
> This sort of history can naturally be linked up with what
> is termed prehistory. The archaeologist collects, classifies,
> and compares the tools and weapons of our ancestors and
> forerunners, examines the houses they built, the fields
> they tilled, the food they ate (or rather discarded). These
> are the tools and instruments of production, characteristic
> of economic systems that no written documents describe.
> (1936a, 7)

Childe applied this model to the archaeological sequences in
the ancient Orient which were interpreted as documenting the
development of man from his first emergence on the planet to a
civilised state. This was seen as a steady upward process in
which man progressively increased his control over non-human
nature. Indeed one of the major aims of the book was to justify
a belief in progress from a scientific standpoint and in the face
of world war and depression. Here it is interesting that as well
as providing him with a model of socio-cultural change, Marxism also suggested to Childe a means of explaining stagnation
in the Orient after the inception of urbanism. Until now Childe
had been primarily concerned to explain culture progress in
Europe and had neglected the equally important question of
decline in the Orient, essential to an overall understanding of
change. Very briefly, Childe argued that the accumulation of
surplus necessary for the inception of urbanism had resulted in
a division of society into classes, a ruling class of kings, priests
and officials and a lower class of peasants and manual labour-
ers. According to Childe, such a social structure was not conducive to further change.

One of the major effects of the class division in Childe's eyes
was the separation of theoretical from practical knowledge. He
argued that while the theoreticians, the kings, the priests, etc.
were members of the upper classes, the craftsmen, exponents
of practical knowledge, were relegated to the lower classes. As
a result the new learning of the upper classes was 'all too often

fettered by subservience to superstition and divorced from the applied sciences that produced results' (1936a, 262). Furthermore he maintained that the priestly class suppressed the motivation for further invention in the craftsmen, whom he considered to have been the pioneers of progress before the revolution.

> Such rulers had few incentives to encourage invention. Many of the revolutionary steps in progress – the harnessing of animals' motive-power, the sail, metal tools – originally appeared as 'labour saving devices'. But the new rulers now commanded almost unlimited reserves of labour recruited from subjects fired with superstitious faith and captives taken in war; they had no need to bother about labour saving inventions. (1936a, 261)

The outcome was a society dominated by magic and superstition. This, he argued, prevented man from further progress through the understanding of nature by practical experimentation.

> The pursuit of the vain hopes and illusory shortcuts suggested by magic and religion repeatedly deterred man from the harder road to the control of Nature by understanding. Magic seemed easier than science, just as torture is less trouble than the collection of evidence.
>
> Magic and religion constituted the scaffolding needed to support the raising structure of social organization and of science. Unhappily the scaffolding repeatedly cramped the execution of the design and impeded the progress of the permanent building. . . . The urban revolution, made possible by science, was exploited by superstition.
> (1936a, 267–8)

Here it should be noted that *Man Makes Himself* constituted a radical departure from the texts hitherto published. *The Dawn*, *The Most Ancient East* and *The Danube in Prehistory* were first and foremost archaeological text-books comprising fairly detailed syntheses of archaeological data within the cultural diffusionist framework. *Man Makes Himself*, however, was essentially a history of man's social evolution from a hunting-gathering stage to civilisation based on the archaeological patterns presented in the earlier texts, yet unencumbered by the detailed discussions undertaken therein.

Interestingly, Trigger (1968, 533) sees the difference between the two types of work as illustrating a tension in Childe's approach between particularising and generalising aims. It is difficult, however, to see in what way either the aims or indeed the texts are incompatible with one another in an overall research strategy. The general works, and here we may include *What Happened in History* (1942) and *The Prehistory of European Society* (1958) were essentially historical interpretations of the data presented in the larger more descriptive texts. Furthermore while the latter were addressed to professional archaeologists and students the former were specifically designed for the bookstall public (1936a, vii ; 1958a, 73). Thus far from illustrating a conflict in Childe's objectives, the two types of work can be seen as complementary pieces of research in an overall enquiry into European and Oriental prehistory.

During Childe's lifetime field research in both Europe and the Near East was being undertaken at an unprecedented rate and Childe was constantly having to revise his texts to keep abreast of new information. By 1939, he felt it necessary to publish another edition of *The Dawn*. Here he reorganised his descriptions of cultural groupings according to a Marxist model of socio-culture, thus introducing a new level of patterning into his work (1958a, 72). While this did not affect the overall framework of the text, it did structure his accounts of individual cultures which had not previously followed any set formula or model. It is significant, however, that although he adopted the Marxist structural analysis of culture, he did not utilise the Marxist theory of socio-cultural change as he had done in *Man Makes Himself*. Unlike the major contemporary Russian archaeologists Childe placed little emphasis on independent evolution as an important causal factor in social change.

To have acknowledged the possibility of independent evolution having occurred in Europe might have provided support to an Occidentalism which, by now, had become little more than a pseudo-scientific justification for the policies of Nazism, a creed repugnant to Childe in all its manifestations. Indeed the misrepresentation of archaeological evidence in Germany led him to conclude :

> Perhaps we are standing at the end of an era of free research. Over a large part of our Continent prehistory has been harnessed to the service of a political dogma. Reliable additions to knowledge there can hardly be expected now. (1939a, xviii)

Whereas previously Childe made it clear that his aim was to balance the role of the Orient and the Occident in the development of European culture, now he makes no mention of this initial objective. He no longer considers the ancient Europeans to have made any positive contribution to the development of modern civilisation, and is concerned only with defending and strengthening the Orientalist hypothesis. This was no simple task since as noted previously neither theory could be substantiated without an independent chronology for prehistoric Europe. Both the short chronology of the Orientalists and the long chronology of the Occidentalists were based on theories which assumed in advance the direction of culture flow between the Orient and Europe. In this context Childe writes

> The long chronology may be gratifying to the local patriotism of North Europeans. Assuming the identity of Battle-axe folk and Indo-Europeans, it relegates the Aryan cradle to the Baltic coasts or Central Germany. For this reason it is on its way to becoming a statutorily sanctioned dogma in Germany – and is suspect scientifically. But this long chronology and its consequences cannot be refuted by any single concrete fact. It is rejected here essentially on the grounds of general probability. (1939a, 327)

Here he introduced an interesting theoretical argument in support of his thesis, in which he compared the patterns of prehistory based on the long and short chronologies with a hypothetical zoning pattern deduced from basic diffusionist principles. It was pointed out previously that one of the most important methodological postulates of diffusionism was the existence of a primary centre of innovation and diffusion. It was generally assumed that the influence of this centre decreased with distance, thus cultures far away from the centre were expected to be of lower cultural status than those nearer it. In this context Childe envisaged a simple pattern comprising a series of cultural zones throughout Europe and the Mediterranean, each possessing a different cultural status according to its distance from the Orient. For the Bronze Age Childe showed how the patterns of prehistory based on both the long and short chronologies agreed with this model.

> Moving from the metropolitan civilizations of Egypt, Babylonia and the Hittite realm at the centre, our map IV discloses:
> 1) Fully-literate city dwellers in peninsular and insular Greece;

2) Illiterate townsmen in Macedonia and Sicily;

3) Sedentary villagers with at least a specialized bronze industry and regular commerce to support it, in the Middle Danube basin, in South-east Spain and perhaps on the Kuban;

4) Less stable communities less highly differentiated, in the Upper Danube basin, Southern and Central Germany, Switzerland, England and South Russia;

5) Self-sufficing neolithic societies in Southern Scandinavia, Northern Germany and Orkney;

6) Groups barely emerging from savagery in the far northern forests.

Even by adopting a long chronology, i.e. by taking the maximal dates for the Oriental ornaments copied in period IV, this picture will not be seriously distorted. Egypt and Mesopotamia, but not Anatolia, retain their capital status. The Aegean world, and with it Sicily, descend one grade in the scale. Central Europe, South-east Spain and Britain still rank as Bronze Age, Scandinavia, and Orkney remain neolithic. But South Russia loses grade.

(1939a, 326, 327)

However for the previous periods Childe argued that only the pattern produced by the short chronology coincided with the classic pattern deduced from the premises of diffusion.

For the earlier periods, the adoption of a long chronology has disconcerting results. The Vardar-Morava continuum must be interpreted as the result of a southward spread of Danubian culture; the Battle-axe cultures must start spontaneously in Central Europe or Denmark, and thence flood the Caucasus, Anatolia and Greece. The spread of megalithic tombs must be reversed so that Minoan tholoi and even Egyptian mastabas become final elaborations of architectural forms created in the barbaric west or north. We are left in period I with neolithic Westerners and Danubians, certainly a stage or two below the contemporary Halafians of Hither Asia and Badarians in Egypt, but no longer connected therewith by recognisable intermediate stages. . . .

Our short chronology preserves for the New Stone Age the same sort of pattern as prehistory (on any chronology), offers in the Bronze Age, and history discloses from the second Iron Age. . . . Moving from the centres of fully literate urban life in Egypt and Mesopotamia map 1 shows;

1) 'Bronze Age' townships in Crete, Anatolia and peninsular Greece.

2) Sedentary neolithic villagers in Thessaly, the Balkans, South-eastern Sicily and South-east Spain.

3) Semi-nomadic self-sufficing peasants on the Danubian löss lands and in Western Europe, including perhaps Southern England.

4) Only food-gatherers on the North European plain and in the northern forests. (1939a, 327, 328)

Childe's argument although quite ingenious is unconvincing. The use of an unverified zonal hypothesis as a standard against which to accept or reject particular patterns of the past is not strictly scientific.

Three years later Childe published his second popular work, *What Happened in History* (1942) in which he traced man's progress from the hunting-gathering stage until the end of the Roman Empire. Written in the third year of World War II Childe at this time held a basically pessimistic view of the future development of European civilisation, believing that it was about to enter another 'Dark Age'. He was determined however not to let this shake his belief in progress and one of the reasons for the enormous geographical and chronological span covered in the book was to achieve an historical perspective on such a 'Dark Age'.

> *What Happened in History* (1942) . . . was a real contribution to archaeology as a concrete and readable demonstration designed for the bookstall public that history as generally understood can be extracted from archaeological data. I wrote it to convince myself that a Dark Age was not a bottomless cleft in which all traditions of culture were finally engulfed. (I was convinced at the time that European Civilization – Capitalist and Stalinist alike – was irrevocably heading for a Dark Age.) So I wrote with more passion and consequently more pretensions to literary style than in my other works. (1958a, 73)

Childe's interest lay only in what he termed 'main stream' cultures, i.e. those which in his eyes made significant contributions to the cultural capital of mankind. His account is centred on the course of the 'main stream' from its source in Egypt and Mesopotamia to its confluence in the Hellenistic

Mediterranean, and while his survey terminates with the fall of the Roman Empire he nevertheless has a clear view of its subsequent course through the feudalims of the Middle Ages to the capitalist economy of modern times (1942a, 31, 32). Thus as Daniel has noted the 'main stream' is little different to the classic patterns of history advanced by nineteenth-century historians.

> It was the stream that came from Greece and Rome and behind those classical lands from Palestine, Babylonia and Egypt. The origin of civilisation and therefore of history was to Childe something that occurred in what he called the Most Ancient East and what Breasted before him had called the Fertile Crescent. (Daniel 1975, 343)

It is, however, significantly different from the pattern suggested in his earlier works. In *The Aryans* he had laid considerable emphasis on the contribution of the prehistoric Europeans, in particular those speaking Indo-European languages, to modern civilisation. As in the first edition of *The Dawn* and in *The Bronze Age* he had indicated a close relationship between the European Bronze Age and modern civilisation, seeing in the former the true foundations of the latter. It is therefore of special interest to consider the place of the European Bronze Age in the context of the main stream analogy.

Previously Childe considered the rapid development of bronze tools and weapons in northern and central Europe to have constituted the most distinctive and progressive feature of European prehistory. But now, analysed from a Marxist viewpoint, he argued that the emergence of a bronze industry in Europe did not solve what he saw as the basic contradictions in the neolithic economy. Childe maintained that shortage of land, due to the uneconomic and extravagant farming techniques of the neolithic peasants, led to competition for land and subsequently the desire for improved weapons. In places this had resulted in the creation of a ruling class extracting surplus from a conquered peasantry in order to pay for bronze metallurgy. The new industry was thus geared to the demands of a warrior aristocracy, and metal was used primarily in a martial context rather than for agricultural or manufacturing purposes. Thus, according to Childe,

> The new bronze industry neither absorbed any appreciable proportion of the surplus rural population, nor equipped it to conquer virgin lands. Pressure on the land

was thus unrelieved. Moreover, at least in Denmark and southern England, the costly bronze armament merely consolidated the authority of ruling groups as did the knight's armour in the Middle Ages. Here Bronze Age burials reveal 'an aristocratic world with a richly developed upper class life based on organized luxury trade and the labour of the lower classes.' (1942a, 157, 158)

Furthermore, he makes no reference to any contribution which the Aryan peoples might have made to the main stream tradition. In fact, at this time, he considered that the parent group could not be identified, either archaeologically or by its physical racial type (1942a, 150). Here he emphasised that the term Aryan should be used in a linguistic sense only referring to the Asiatic branch of the Indo-European language group. In this context, he totally dismissed the Nazi use of the term. 'As used by Nazis and anti-Semites generally, the term "Aryan" means as little as the words "Bolshie" and "Red" in the mouths of crusted Tories' (1942a, 150).

While Childe is not explicit about his changed viewpoint, it is relatively easy to infer the reasons behind it. Writing in the third year of the war, he had seen the consequences of unsubstantiated speculation supporting the idealogical convictions of Nazism. A natural revulsion from Hitlerism had led him to reject Occidentalism in any form (1958a, 72).

In *What Happened in History*, as in *Man Makes Himself*, Childe adopted an explicitly Marxist interpretation of the archaeological record, inasmuch as he stressed the important role of the economic basis of society in influencing the sociological and ideological superstructures. As in the 1939 edition of *The Dawn*, however, the adoption of a Marxist analysis coincided with a consolidation of his Oriental diffusionism. At a time when the orthodox Soviet line was strongly evolutionist this was a rather paradoxical position for a Marxist to take. Never, even in his most avowedly Marxist phase, did Childe follow the contemporary Russian example and abandon diffusion as a mechanism of change. Three years later in his introduction to a conference on the 'Problems and Prospects of European Archaeology' he makes it clear that he saw the Russian approach as a reaction against the ideology of imperialism rather than as an understanding of the work of Engels or Marx (1945d, 6).

As a result of closer contact with the U.S.S.R. during the war years, Childe did however become more sympathetic towards the Soviet view of culture change. This shift in his attitude is perhaps best illustrated in two works published in the immediate post-war years, *Scotland Before the Scots* (1946) and the fourth edition of *The Dawn* (1947). In neither case did he alter his basic diffusionist stance but in both he exhibits a willingness to admit the possibility of alternative theories of culture change.

In continental Europe, the main change in his argument was in the context of the Battle-axe cultures. Previously he had considered the cultural similarities linking these to be the result of the migration and invasion of warrior pastoralists from south Russia through central Europe to north-west Germany. Now, since he was more open to the Russian argument that the internal development of society was a major factor in culture change, he could also better appreciate the Russian view of the development of the Battle-axe cultures, while not wholly accepting it. In contrast to the migration-invasionist thesis advanced in the west, Soviet archaeologists emphasised the cultural continuity in the development of European society, illustrating precedents for the Battle-axe cultures in Danubian II and even in the Mesolithic hunter-gatherers. In this context, they argued that the similarities existing between various groupings of Battle-axe cultures could have been transmitted during the normal intercourse which takes place between highly mobile bands of pastoralists. While Childe was impressed by this argument he did not consider that the development of the Battle-axe cultures could be wholly explained without recourse to external influences.

> The Soviet account is certainly more economical of undemonstrable assumptions than any migrationist interpretation. But there are difficulties in Krichevskii's version that the Battle-axe cultures arose out of Danubian and Black-earth peasant cultures as a result of purely internal social development. . . .

> This development could hardly be understood without reference to external stimuli. No hunter-fishers on their own could have started breeding sheep or cultivating cereals in Denmark, Sweden or Central Russia where no sheep nor cereals grew wild. The stone battle-axes were derived from antler axes, not so much directly as through metal translations. Food production and metal were alike

introduced in most of the battle-axe provinces. But introduction need not imply migration, but only diffusion.
(1947a, 174, 175)

Apart from this modification however, the 1947 edition of *The
Dawn* was very similar to its predecessor of 1939, presenting
the same zonal argument in favour of the Orientalist position.

Childe maintained this Orientalist stance throughout the remaining years of the forties and the early years of the fifties,
and both *Prehistoric Migrations* (1950) and the chapter in *The
European Inheritance* (1954) edited by Barker, Clark and Vaucher were dominated 'by an old fashioned over-estimation of
the Orient's role' (1958a, 73). In the middle of the decade,
however, he returned dramatically to his original viewpoint
concerning the progressive character of the European Bronze
Age.

> European societies were never passive recipients of Orien-
> tal contributions, but displayed more originality and in-
> ventiveness in developing Oriental inventions than had
> the inventors' more direct heirs in Egypt and Hither Asia.
> This is most obvious in the Bronze Age of Temperate
> Europe. In the Near East many metal types persisted
> unchanged for two thousand years; in Temperate Europe
> an extraordinarily brisk evolution of tools and weapons
> and multiplication of types occupied a quarter of that
> time. (1957a, 342–3)

In this context he emphasised as before

> that even in prehistoric times barbarian societies in
> Europe behaved in a distinctly European way, fore-
> shadowing, however dimly, the contrast with African or
> Asiatic societies that has become manifest in the last
> thousand years. (1958b, 9)

His analysis of the situation, however, is radically different
from that presented in the earlier works, where he had attributed a major role to the Aryan peoples in the foundation of both
the European Bronze Age and modern civilisation. Now he
insisted that

> the explanation must of course be sociological not bio-
> logical. Science, like technology is the creation of societies
> not races; its precepts and results are transmitted by social
> tradition, not 'in the blood'. (1958b, 9)

Childe himself, of course, had not advanced a 'biological'

explanation of progress in Europe. On the contrary, he had taken considerable care to differentiate between his own linguistic hypothesis and a racialist one. Nevertheless his view of the Aryans as 'founders of Western Civilization' was not significantly different from that of the Germanists, and it was, no doubt, the similarity of his analysis to that exploited by the Nazi party during the thirties and early forties that led him to reject the thesis in its entirety.

Childe's return to his original view of the European Bronze Age was thus not a return to his original philological thesis. Now his argument is firmly based on his economic interpretation of the Bronze Age as expounded as early as 1930. Basically, Childe had argued that bronze working required full-time specialisation and thus the liberation of certain members of society from the food-producing processes. This, he had emphasised, could only be achieved by the accumulation of a surplus food supply. In *Man Makes Himself* and in *What Happened in History* he had gone on to show how in the Orient this surplus had been concentrated in the hands of divine kings or priest-kings and the members of a small aristocratic class. However, while he considered that such a social structure was essential in bringing about the new economy he argued that it inhibited further technological progress.

In *The Prehistory of European Society* (1958) Childe upheld the main points in this argument. As before he emphasised that with the division of society into classes, the craftsman was not only reduced to the lower class, but to utter dependence on the state for both his food and raw materials (1958b, 93). This, he suggested, not only relieved the craftsmen of responsibility for decision making but deprived them of a market for labour-saving devices and so of all stimulus for fresh inventions.

> Now a prehistoric metal-worker presumably would have no difficulty in persuading of the superiority of metal weapons or tools his fellow-clansmen or his war-chief, who would have to use them. It would be quite another matter to convince a divine king whose active participation in combat is enormously exaggerated in his monuments, while clerks wielding pens would not be interested in saws or sickles. At the same time the peasantry were so thoroughly stripped of surplus produce, that is, of purchasing power, that they could not afford metal tools. (1958b, 95)

Similarly he stressed that the class division had important ideological consequences, bringing about not only the separation of theoretical from practical knowledge but the devaluation of the latter.

> Finally, the relegation of craftsmen to the lower class excluded them from literacy and isolated the pure sciences of Egyptian and Sumerian clerks from the applied sciences of miners, smelters, smiths and potters. Craft lore could not be committed to writing but continued to be handed on by precept and example. Just for this reason it remained empirical and particular while learned science was not fertilized by experience gained in workshop practice. (1958b, 96)

A society controlled by divine kings or priests gave little emphasis to 'Custom', i.e. 'the society's collective experience, the wisdom gathered and tested by ancestral generations, the science of the period' (1958b, 93, 94). This became replaced by 'laws and regulations imposed on Society by – or in the name of – gods above and outside Society' (1958b, 94). Thus according to Childe the society was dominated by an elite whose knowledge of the world had not been gained by practical experimentation and was thus in his eyes of limited value. It was this ascendancy of magic and religion over the applied sciences that he believed prohibited further technological progress.

Childe maintained that the Bronze Age economy emerged in Europe in a different manner and thus had different results. As early as 1925, he had argued that the peoples of the Aegean were the first Europeans to be affected by the growth of civilisation in the Orient, seeing the diffusion of urbanism from the latter region as the result of a number of processes: war, trade, migration, etc. At this time, while he had emphasised the progressive character of Aegean culture, stressing its European, as opposed to Oriental, 'spirit', he had offered no explanation for this (1925a, 29). Now, however, he put forward an argument in support of this viewpoint. As before he envisaged the actual immigration of craftsmen from the ancient civilisations of Egypt and Mesopotamia.

> Let us admit that prospectors from the older centres of civilization had discovered the lodes of ore and other raw material whose value had first been apreciated in the Near East. Let us admit that coppersmiths, goldsmiths, seal-engravers and other artisans had emigrated to the Aegean

coasts. In neither case had they arrived as agents of a
foreign state or as emissaries of alien profit-making concerns. The hypothetical prospectors no doubt would and
could have come only because they were assured of a
certain market in Egypt and Mesopotamia. (1958b, 111)

What is new, however, is his understanding of the economic
and sociological context of the rise of urbanism in the area. He
argues that since the peoples of the Aegean could draw on
Oriental surplus by use of their raw materials, mercenaries,
raids and piracy, they were able to develop a bronze industry
without submitting to the repressive social structure of Oriental
civilisation.

The Urban Revolution in Greece and Crete had not
created a single State capable of restricting free movement
of individuals. It had created a number of virtually independent kinglets, each rich enough to be a generous
patron. (1958b, 157)

Thus for Childe the emergence of the new economy in the
Aegean did not create an impassive economic gulf that divided
society into irrevocably opposing classes. Although there is
some evidence for a division between rich and poor, wealth
seems to be more evenly distributed. 'Judging by the contents
of private tombs, quite a generous share must have been dis-
persed through a broad middle-class of townsfolk and "com-
panions"' (1958b, 161). Furthermore it was in this class that
Childe placed the Aegean craftsman, favourably contrasting
his position with that of his Oriental counterpart. Finally,
whereas he had come to view the Oriental market as not
conducive to change, he considered the opposite to be true of
the Aegean commercial system.

Early Aegean craftsmen were producing for an international market and not just to satisfy demands constituted by the traditional tastes and habits of a single society.
Each community would develop divergent fashions and
working practices. A craftsman should adjust his techniques and his output to the consequent local variations of
demand. Thus he was encouraged not merely to maintain
a fixed standard of technical competence . . . but also to
introduce innovations that should by their efficiency or
beauty attract discriminating purchasers. (1958b, 113)

Nevertheless, despite its progressive elements, Aegean civilisation, like Oriental civilisation declined and eventually col-

lapsed. In Childe's eyes,

> Too much real capital was squandered in destructive dynastic struggles of which the legendary Trojan war was just the culmination. Barbarian hordes, some at least exploited and trained by Myceneans, after annihilating Hittite civilization and ravaging cities of the Levant, eventually finished off the Mycenean civilization, rotten with internal contradictions. The half-legendary Dorian Invasion finally plunged the Aegean world into a Dark Age.
> (1958b, 161)

As Renfrew (1973, 99) has pointed out, Childe's argument for the beginnings of a central European Bronze Age was in most respects the exact counterpart of his theory for the origins of Aegean civilisation. Just as he had envisaged Oriental prospectors establishing a bronze industry in the Aegean, now he saw metallurgists from the latter region founding a European industry. Similarly, precisely as he had emphasised the Aegean industry's initial dependence on Oriental capital, now he stressed the European debt to Minoan–Mycenean surplus.

> The Aegean surplus . . . served as the foundation for a bronze industry in Temperate Europe in which Aegean traditions of craftsmanship could operate freely. . . . The commercial system thus disclosed had been called into being to supply the Aegean market: it was the accumulated resources of the Minoan–Mycenean civilization that guaranteed to the distributors a livelihood, indeed an adequate recompense, for the hazards and hardships of their travels. . . . In the Early Bronze Age peninsular Italy, Central Europe, the West Baltic coastlands, and the British Isles were united by a single system for the distribution of metalware, rooted in the Aegean market.
> (1958b, 161–6)

Although he inferred economic unity, Childe insisted that this did not entail any political or cultural agreement. On the contrary, he laid considerable emphasis on the diversity and variation existing within European society at this time. Here he envisaged a multiplicity of ethnic groups, ranging from nomadic pastoralists to agricultural villagers, all ultimately based on a mixed farming economy. While in most cultures he saw no explicit evidence for the concentration of political and economic power either by chiefs or gods, in a few instances such as Wessex he inferred the existence of rich aristocracies. In this context he considered that only a few societies could produce the amount of surplus required to support a resident smith. As a result Childe postulated that the metallurgists were forced outside the kinship structure of tribal society. While this was perhaps detrimental to their personal security, it gave them a freedom not enjoyed by either their Aegean or Oriental counterparts.

> In any case despite all disabilities European metalworkers were free. They were not tied to any one patron or even to a single tribal society. (1958b, 169)

Childe believed that it was this freedom of the metallurgist, together with the nature of the market he was producing for, which explained the rapid development of the European bronze industry.

> A market of this kind offered every inducement to originality on the part of the producers. At the same time their very itineracy and far-flung commercial contacts should fertilize native genius. They met on the frontiers of their territories colleagues working to satisfy the divergent tastes of other societies and perhaps employing ores or metals of different composition. Among the wares they handled they would see products of more distant schools of metal-work for comparison with familiar local types. Thus the peculiar structure of the European bronze industry induced an effective pooling of experiences, gained in different environments, and of traditions evoked by divergent popular tasts. As a result European bronze workers did display inventiveness and ingenuity to an exceptional degree. (1958b, 169, 170)

As he had done initially, Childe now inferred a close relationship between Bronze Age society in Europe and modern western civilisation.

> In temperate Europe by 1500 B.C. had been established a distinctive politico-economic structure such as had existed a thousand years earlier in the Aegean, but nowhere else in the Bronze Age world. . . . The author had neither the space nor the knowledge at his disposal to show in detail how closely this Bronze Age system foreshadowed the peculiarities of European polity in Antiquity, the Middle Ages and Modern Times. Obviously all the essential features outlined above were replicated in Classical Greece. Slavery and totalitarianism temporarily distorted the pat-

tern within the Hellenistic monarchies and the Roman
Empire. But barbarian Europe outside their frontiers was
a direct continuation of Bronze Age Europe as just described. . . . The national states that eventually emerged
were indeed enormously larger than our Bronze Age
tribes and fewer in number. But they have all shown
themselves just as mutually jealous in policy and as com-
petitive economically. All have been increasingly dependent on a supra-national economic system for vital raw
materials as well as the disposal of their own products.
(1958b, 172, 173)

Here Childe made the interesting suggestion that throughout
this time the craftsmen, the exponents of the applied sciences,
preserved their traditional freedom of movement within the
supranational economy. In this context he added,

The metics at Athens, the way-faring journeymen of the
Middle Ages, and the migrant craft unionist of the nineteenth century are the lineal descendants of the itinerants
just described. But so were the Natural Philosophers and
Sophists in Classical Greece, the travelling scholars of
medieval Europe, and the natural scientists who from the
days of Galileo and Newton to 1945 freely exchanged
information and ideas by publication, correspondence,
and visits regardless of political frontiers. (1958b, 173)

By preserving their freedom outwith the tribal or national
frontiers, the craftsmen and their 'lineal descendants' were
allowed to advance their knowledge of the world unrestricted
by contemporary social structures. And since in Childe's eyes
this understanding was the essential prerequisite of technological invention, it offered him an explanation of the rapid technological progress of European society.

From 'Retrospect' it would seem that Childe was in two
minds concerning *The Prehistory of European Society*. While
he was aware that his argument rested on insecure foundations,
he was nevertheless enthusiastic about his overall approach.

Now I confess that my whole account may prove to be
erroneous; my formulae may be inadequate; my interpretations are perhaps ill-founded, my chronological framework – and without such one cannot speak of conjunc-
tures – is frankly shaky. Yet I submit the result was worth
publishing. It is a final answer to those who told us: 'the
true prelude to European history was written in Egypt,

Mesopotamia and Palestine while the natives of Europe remained illiterate barbarians.' It exemplifies better than any other work I know how what everyone will accept as history could be extracted from archaeological finds; whether the particular extract be accepted or no, it should help to confirm the status of archaeology among historical disciplines. At the same time it illustrates what scientific history ought in my opinion to be like. (1958a, 74)

Finally, while he does not draw attention to the fact, Childe had at last found a possible explanation for the creativity of European society which was sociological and could not be interpreted in racial terms. As noted previously, while Childe had never advanced a racist thesis, his initial emphasis on the superiority of the language and intellect of the Aryans was uncomfortably close to the German doctrine of genetic superiority.

Certainly in 'Retrospect' he did not wish to draw attention to his original philological thesis. In fact he was even reluctant to admit to his early recognition of the distinctive quality of the European Bronze Age, implying that this was a comparatively recent realisation.

In rewriting *New Light on the Most Ancient East* in 1954 and *The Dawn of European Civilization* in 1956, I began to realize how right Hawkes had been in 1940 when in his *The Prehistoric Foundations of Europe* he had insisted that by the Bronze Age, Europe had achieved a kind of culture distinctively of its own. I saw not only that this was so but also why. (1958a, 74)

Childe was thus apparently so unwilling to admit to his early philological thesis that he misrepresented his own intellectual genesis and development. He did not, as he suggested in 'Retrospect', start off a confirmed Orientalist and only in his later works achieve a more balanced view of European prehistory. In fact he began by attempting to achieve a synthesis between Oriental diffusion and the independent evolution of European culture. It was during the thirties that he came firmly down in the Orientalist camp, and in doing so rejected his original synthesis. In the fifties, then, Childe's recognition of the creative quality of the European Bronze Age was not a new realisation but rather a true recognition in the sense of a knowing again.

What was immediately striking about this final analysis was

its hypothetical status. As Piggott commented with reference to the role of the Bronze Age metallurgist, 'this technological emancipation is no more than an assumption, in its very nature impossible to document in archaeological terms' (1965, 126). While we might not go as far as this in limiting archaeological inference, certainly it is true that Childe offered no evidence from the archaeological record to support his view of the metallurgist or his 'lineal descendants' in contributing to progress in Europe. Neither did he convincingly substantiate his argument that the development of the European Bronze industry was only possible because of the immigration of Oriental craftsmen and the injection of Oriental capital into the European economies. Childe, then, offered a socio-economic analysis of the European Bronze Age and its relationship to modern civilisation, but was unable to verify it in the archaeological record.

Today, of course, it is not only Childe's final interpretation of the European Bronze Age which has been brought into question, but also certain fundamental links in his structure of European prehistory, together with the diffusionist assumptions at the heart of his thesis (Renfrew 1973). With the tree-ring calibration of radiocarbon dates for prehistoric Europe a new pattern is emerging which illustrates the chronological precedence of many European cultures over their assumed parent cultures in the eastern Mediterranean. Indeed Renfrew has distinguished a 'fault line' which snaps the basic chronological and cultural links between Europe and the Orient. Childe's framework has collapsed. As Renfrew (1973, 19) has emphasised, European prehistory will have to be rewritten, a task which will require years of work by many scholars.

2

The Concept of Culture

Archaeology as a relatively new discipline is confronted with a legacy of terms and concepts that it did not generate but which were imported from other disciplines where they often had a quite different referent. The terms 'epoch' or 'age' and 'type-fossil' are obvious examples. Derived from a geological model they carried with them into archaeology connotations and implications that, while valid in a geological context, were not wholly suited to the nature of archaeological data. The resultant confusions between chronological and spatial patterns in European prehistory and between absolute and relative time are well known.

The term culture is another perhaps less obvious borrowing, being imported from the social rather than the natural sciences. Although given a specifically archaeological definition and function by Childe (1929, v, vi) it has never been entirely freed from its broader anthropological overtones. And here it is important to note that while type-fossil and epoch had clearly defined meanings in geology, this was never the case with the badly over-taxed term culture which during its history has encompassed a wide variety of meanings and usages (Kroeber and Kluckholn 1952).

At its root the term embraces the Latin verb *colere* meaning to cultivate or tend. Initially this was applied in a purely agricultural context, but even in ancient times it came to be used with regard to the mind, body and the Gods (Lewis and Short 1966, 369). In its first applications in English during the sixteenth and seventeenth centuries the primary notion of cultivation was retained but it was also applied to the mind and the body (Oxford English Dictionary 1933, ii 1249). By the beginning of the nineteenth century a secondary concept had emerged which referred to a high degree of cultivation of the mind and refinement in taste and manners. This was also, as Kroeber and Kluckholn (1952, 11–18) have pointed out, the older meaning of the term civilisation, which is the nearest synonym to culture. In archaeological literature during the nineteenth century the term was employed primarily in an Oriental and Aegean context where it was used synonymously with civilisation as denoting the general way of life of a people, or as representing a stage in the growth of civilisation (Daniel 1975, 242–3).

With the impact of Darwinism on the study of man in the second half of the nineteenth century, a new theoretical dimension was introduced into the culture concept. Now it came to specify that category of phenomena, both material and non-material, which had been acquired through a process of social vis-à-vis biological evolution. The first use of the term in this sense is usually attributed to E. B. Tylor in *Primitive Culture* (1871)

> Culture or Civilization, taken in its wide ethnographic sense, is that complex whole which includes knowledge, belief, art, morals, law, custom and any other capabilities and habits acquired by man as a member of society.
> (Tylor 1871, 1)

This view of culture provided the basis for many subsequent definitions in the twentieth century. These are too numerous and varied to name (see Kroeber and Kluckhohn 1952; Harris 1968), but very broadly they can be divided into two major categories. First, those where culture is viewed as all non-biologically acquired characteristics, i.e. both material and non-material; and secondly where culture is restricted to the mental or ideational plane. According to this latter view, material extrasomatic items are cultural products – not the culture itself. Because of the emphasis on shared ideas, values and beliefs, i.e. 'norms', Binford (1972b, 125) has termed this the normative school.

In addition to these holistic senses 'culture' is also widely employed on a partitive level to refer to particular organisational units, i.e. extrasomatic traits of specific human groups.

The introduction of the concept of culture into archaeology is generally considered to be a major turning point in the history of the discipline (Daniel 1962, 16ff.; *idem* 1975, 236–51). With the new concept archaeologists were able to transcend the limitations of a purely epochal model of the past – the pattern of prehistory could be seen not solely as vertical series of epochs but as having a horizontal as well as vertical component. In other words culture introduced a new spatial dynamic into the classification and interpretation of material remains. Just as important for the adherents of the new concept was the access which they believed it afforded to the 'people' behind the data. A new and exciting vision of prehistory was emerging in which prehistoric groups were seen to weave intricate patterns with one another across time-space continua which had previously been considered uniform epochs.

It is thus interesting that during the twenties the importance of the transition from the epochal to the cultural paradigm was not made wholly explicit by the exponents of the new concept. As Trigger (1978, 83) has pointed out neither Crawford (1921) nor Peake (1922) saw the need to define the term. Burkitt (1923, 18) on the other hand, applied it to a grouping of archaeological remains which was larger than an industry but not yet a civilisation. Childe himself employed the term as the classificatory basis of three of his major texts, *The Dawn of European Civilization* (1925), The Aryans (1926) and *The Most Ancient East* (1928) without any prior discussion as to meaning. Considering the novelty of the concept at the time, this lack of definition illustrates a less conscious attitude towards theory than that prevailing in the discipline today.

Indeed it was not until 1929 in a brief statement on archaeological procedure in the Preface to *The Danube in Prehistory* that Childe first defined the term. Here he limited its field of application to a material level only, i.e. as a unit of classification for archaeological remains.

> We find certain types of remains – pots, implements, ornaments, burial rites and house forms – constantly recurring together. Such a complex of associated traits we shall term a 'cultural group' or just a 'culture'. We assume that such a complex is the material expression of what today would be called a 'people'. Only where the complex in question is regularly and exclusively associated with the skeletal remains of a specfic physical type would we venture to replace 'people' by the term 'race'.
>
> (1929, v, vi)

He thus introduced a new and discrete usage of the term which was significantly different from current anthropological usage. Unlike the latter which embraced a theory of non-biological or social inheritance, Childe's usage was purely a classificatory device for ordering archaeological data. While he did not acknowledge it at the time, Childe later made it clear that he derived this specifically archaeological usage of the term from German prehistorians, in particular from Gustav Kossinna, his main rival in the field of Aryan philology.

It was . . . in Northern Europe and especially in Germany . . . that archaeologists first came to see clearly that assemblages of type fossils might characterise not only distinct periods of time, but also distinct nations or tribes within a single period. And it was German prehistorians who first came to term such recurrent assemblages of type-fossils 'Kulturen'. . . . It was formed explicitly before the end of the nineteenth century by Gustav Kossinna, a philologist and Germanist who turned from the humanities to archaeology.

'Sharply defined archaeological culture provinces coincide at all times with quite definite peoples or tribes, cultural regions are ethnic regions, cultural groups are peoples.' (1956a, 28)

When Childe first formulated his definition he made the important assumption that the archaeologist's culture coincided with a 'people' and only in cases of skeletal homogeneity with a 'race'. Childe did not attempt to define either of these terms, but from the context it is clear that he is basically contrasting a social with a biological grouping. Here it should be noted that at the time this restriction of the term race to its scientific meaning was unusual. During the twenties and thirties it was widely employed to encompass socio-economic, political and even religious groupings. Such extension in meaning was symptomatic not only of the widespread confusion concerning the nature of both biological and social evolution, but also of the rise of racialism in western Europe.

During the early thirties Childe became very concerned about the misapplication of archaeological, anthropological and philological theory to support the racialist policies of Nazi Germany. As illustrated in the previous chapter this resulted in his rejection of the Aryan thesis of progress and in his denial of the progressive quality of the European Bronze Age itself. At the same time it led him to look more closely at the specialised terms employed in archaeology and related disciplines with view to clarifying their meaning and explicating the underlying assumptions. In 'Races, Peoples and Cultures in Prehistoric Europe' (1933) Childe pleaded for a rigorous scientific definition of the term race as a group of persons all sharing perceptible and measurable peculiarities that have been and can be inherited. And in this context he outlined the difficulties involved in the classification of racial groupings in prehistory.

> Living men are usually classified racially according to stature, head-form, shape of the nose, colour of the skin, eyes and hair, extent and quality of the hair, and so on. But from ancient times only skeletons, and they generally fragmentary, are preserved. Comparatively few of the features used to differentiate between living races can be recognised on such material. In practice only head-form, stature, and in favourable cases the shape of the nose, are available. And stature has been shown now to be rather a matter of diet than of stable hereditary factors. (1933b, 195)

Here he warned that the simple classification of skulls into dolichocephalic and brachycephalic, i.e. long and round heads in fact masked the diversity of prehistoric populations and was thus of only limited value.

For Childe the salient feature of a 'people' was that it was a social grouping. He was unconcerned at the time to give an exact definition of the term according to a fixed set of criteria but clearly saw it as encompassing different types of social groups, illustrating this by two concrete examples, the English people and the Jewish people.

> The English people includes representatives of three distinct layers of prehistoric invaders as well as of Anglo-Saxons, Danes, Normans, Flemings and later arrivals. But all now share, besides a common language and common institutions, quite a number of peculiarities in material culture, such as baths and water closets. In the same way the Jews are a people. Despite their comparative segregation and consequent inbreeding they do not all conform to a single physical type; indeed three distinct stocks have been distinguished. . . . Community of traditions and language has united all these distinct stocks into a single people, but not yet into a physical race. (1933b, 198, 199)

It would thus seem that Childe considered a 'people' to represent a single society, though not necessarily corresponding to a single political system, to be a linguistic unit and to have a common social tradition. At the same time, it should be noted that his example of the Jewish people was not without significant political overtones. If the Jews were a social and not a racial grouping, the racialist policies being undertaken against them in Nazi Germany could be attacked on theoretical as well as humanitarian grounds.

As in *The Danube in Prehistory*, Childe defined the prehistorians' culture as a grouping of associated traits found in the archaeological record, this time differentiating between what he terms 'material' and 'spiritual' components.

> Prehistoric archaeology for its part has, particularly since the war, been working with the concept of a 'culture'. It finds that groups of distinctive traits, mostly pecularities in material culture (dress, armament, ornaments, domestic architecture), but also more spiritual characteristics such as burial rites and artistic styles, tend to hang together and be associated in a given continuous region at a given period. Such a group of associated traits is what the archaeologist terms a *culture*.
>
> (1933b, 197, 198; my emphasis)

The choice of the term 'material culture' to apply to a subcomponent of the archaeologist's culture is unfortunate since the latter is by his own definition 'the material expression of what today would be termed a people' (1929, vi). Obviously he is using the term 'material' in two different senses.

In 'Is Prehistory Practical?' (1933) Childe again stressed the need for a scientific definition of the terms employed in archaeology and related disciplines. This was important to him, and here he was very explicit, since he was deeply concerned about the use of what he termed 'the supposed facts of Prehistory' (1933a, 410) to support the racialist programme of the third Reich in Germany.

> The suppression of thought during the Dark Ages was justified by an appeal to supposed revelations, vouchsafed to individuals, and the interpretations thereof. The latest onslaught on the freedom of the spirit appeals to alleged scientific facts. The justificatory documents this time actually exist in the public world – in museums and in the fields – open to every competent observer to examine, analyze and compare. But these documents can no more be profitably studied without laborious preparatory training than can the movement of stars or the behaviour of electrons. Prehistory in its several branches is just the objective and critical study of precisely those data upon

which the political theories of Houston Chamberlain and Adolf Hitler purport to be built. But for the purpose of such systematic study the several sciences that compose Prehistory have had to elaborate an exact terminology, and in doing so have often defined a given term in a different way to vulgar speech and sometimes even differently to colleagues in allied disciplines. The layman may well be pardoned if he takes these technical terms at their face value, but the resultant confusion may have disastrous effects. (1933a, 410)

It is perhaps ironical, however, that despite his avowed conern with rigorous definition, Childe himself was guilty of the linguistic ambiguity which he so strongly condemned. While he clearly advanced a biological definition of race, rejecting its indiscriminate application to linguistic, political and religious groupings, he was not so clear in his usage of the term culture. Previously he had defined it in a specifically archaeological sense to refer to groupings of relics and monuments which the archaeologist discerns in the archaeological record. At face value this was purely a taxonomic unit for material remains. It did not encompass an explanation of how these material traits came to be grouped together, i.e. by social rather than biological means. Here, however, it is precisely this thesis of extrasomatic acquisition which sustains his definition of culture.

As a protection against cold or enemies the other animals have to rely upon the fur or the horns conferred upon them by heredity (in the biological sense). Man alone can kindle fire and manufacture clothes to keep him warm, can fabricate weapons for his defense. These things – fire, clothes, weapons – are part of man's 'culture', external to his body, to be made and discarded at will. He only acquires them after birth, whereas a tendency to grow fur and claws is innate in a cat which cannot discard them at will. Only by mutations in the germ plasm could a better equipped animal arise, which as a result of processes of natural selection might become after many generations the parent of a new race or even species. (1933a, 412)

As well as embracing a theory of non-biological inheritance this view of culture differs from Childe's earlier definition in that it is a holistic as opposed to a partitive concept, i.e. it does not refer to a particular unit but rather to a general class of phenomena (of non-biologically acquired characteristics). Childe, however, did not explicitly differentiate this broader meaning of the term culture from his archaeological definition. Indeed he seemed to regard it as implicit in the latter definition, using it as support for his equation between the archaeological unit and a 'people'.

> In the prehistoric past as obviously today, culture was independent of physical race, was not a matter of biological heredity but of social tradition.

> Ignorance of this fact, or rather the careless use of the word race as coloured by biological theory for the prehistoric group distinguished by a peculiar culture, has naturally reinforced the false analogy between man and poultry in misleading 'racial hygienists' and their political interpreters. If we replace the word 'race' in this context by 'people' we shall more easily avoid such confusions. (1933a, 417)

Childe then was content to use the term culture simultaneously in two quite different senses, without either clearly differentiating between their discrete usages or explicitly discussing their relationship. In an article expressly concerned with the definition of technical terms, it illustrates a significant blindspot in his approach. What it shows is that his concern with definition was not fundamental but restricted to the issue of race. This was of such pressing practical importance to him that it diverted his attention from other terminological problems. It was only much later in his career that he was to look in any depth at the various meanings of culture.

In 1935, in 'Changing Methods and Aims in Prehistory', his presidential address to the Prehistoric Society, Childe presented a novel approach to the culture concept. Here he introduced what he termed a functional interpretation of culture, where culture is viewed 'not as a dead group of fossils or curios but as a living functioning organism' (1935c, 10). This was a method of approach which he gained from contemporary anthropological theory.

> The study of living human societies as functioning organisms has revealed to archaeologists this approach to their materials. It has led to the correct definition and interpretation of the concept of culture. (1935c, 3)

Childe had always kept in close contact with the theoretical developments in anthropology which he considered to be the

sister discipline of archaeology in the science of man (1946d).
Functionalism had risen primarily as a reaction against the
controversy raging between the Evolutionists and Diffusionists. Denying the value of the speculative reconstruction of
history, functionalists emphasised the need to study existing
societies, intensive field research comprising a major part of
their programme. An important aspect of their approach to
cultural analysis was the employment of the analogy between
organic structure and social structure, an old analogy which
goes back at least to Hobbes and finds its fullest elaboration in
Spencer (Harris 1968, 526). Functionalists, then, tended to
stress the unity of the cultural system and to emphasise the
interrelationship between the different components in that
system.

In Britain there were two major schools of functionalist
thought, one represented by Radcliffe-Brown and the other by
Malinowski. Whereas the former tended to concentrate their
attention on social structure, the latter studied all aspects of
society (Harris 1968, 514–67). Where Childe admitted a debt
to functionalism was in his use of the concept of adaptation.
Even here, however, his approach was distinctly Childean, for
unlike either Radcliffe-Brown or Malinowski, it was the
'material culture' which he saw to have the main adaptive
potential.

> Tools and cultivation plots, vessels and hut-foundations
> reveal the equipment used by the community in the daily
> business of securing food and shelter; the techniques of
> their manufacture and cultivation reveal the science, the
> collective experience that the group is applying to those
> ends. We see material culture as an adaptation to an
> environment, to use a biological term. (1935c, 10)

While he was aware that the 'spiritual culture' might aid the
survival of the group by promoting social cohesiveness, he
acknowledged that it might also play a counter-productive role.
In other words he believed that not every cultural phenomenon
need be adaptive.

> The archaeologist is not entirely restricted to material
> culture, his material includes items which must be assigned
> to the domain of spiritual culture. Amulets and megalithic
> tombs, sculptures in the round and designs painted on
> vases have no obvious utility; from the materialist stand-
> point they did not help their makers and builders to get

more food or to rear more offspring. Their makers may indeed have hoped to obtain such results. And functional anthropology will show how ritual and art by promoting social solidarity or dispelling anxieties contributed to a group's survival. But a rationalist will demonstrate no less plausibly how superstitions hinder material progress and indeed precipitated disasters. (1935c, 14)

The functionalist emphasis on adaptation has been restated by an influential school of archaeologists who would go so far as including it within their definition of culture as an axiomatic premise (Binford 1972b, 127). As Childe pointed out adaptation is basically a biological concept. Indeed it has a very specific meaning within the precise theoretical framework of post-Darwinian biology. In this context an adaptation is defined as a genetic change which confers a reproductive advantage on the organism. Such an adaptive or advantageous change thus in time becomes prevalent in the in-breeding population or species through genetic transmission and has thus been 'selected' by nature. Biological adaptation can thus be estimated numerically.

In 'Changing Methods and Aims' Childe suggested that one might evaluate 'material culture' change according to this strict biological criterion.

> The function of the animal's bodily equipment is to enable it to live and propagate its species. Material culture, as defined here, is just the assemblage of devices that a community has invented or learnt to enable it to survive and expand . . . success in survival, expressible in numerical terms measures the biological value of a species' inherited endowments. The same standard should apply to material culture. Advances in material culture should promote a numerical increase in the community that creates or adopts them. (1935c, 11)

For Childe the advantage of a purely quantitative definition of success was that it was value-free and thus in his eyes scientific (1936a, 12ff.). Judged by this standard the industrial revolution was clearly a success.

> It has facilitated the survival and multiplication of the species concerned. The figures provide an objective criterion by which such an event may be judged. It is useless to insist either on the lustre of intellectual achievements in science which the new system of production alone

made possible, or the horrors of child-labour, slums and the oppression which accompanied it. (1936a, 15, 16)

Interestingly, however, Childe was never able to reconcile himself completely to a purely quantitative definition of success even in the realms of biological evolution. This was brought out by his extreme unwillingness to equate organisms lower on the evolutionary scale whose numbers have been maintained or increased over the millennia with higher organisms such as man whose numbers have also increased (1936a, 13, 14)

This displays a reluctance on Childe's part to let go of the value-loaded connotations implicit in the term success as employed in everyday language. Again we can see the same problem, a term with a variety of referents being defined in a very specific manner, yet being employed simultaneously with overtones of its other meanings. Value laden terms such as success and progress (see chapter 4) are particularly prone to misinterpretation if they are given meanings quite different to their everyday usage and read by someone unfamiliar with that particular contextual usage.

At this time Childe emphasised that it was not enough to describe the cultural group without reference to its external context, 'to see the culture functioning the environment to which it was an adaptation must be reconstructed' (1935c, 10). Here he was thinking primarily in terms of the geophysical environment. Later he was to become aware that this was too simplistic a notion.

> The ambiguous use of the term 'adaptation' is too well-recognised to prevent the formula being a serviceable heuristic instrument. But is the word 'environment' used less ambiguously? (1949a, 6)

In *Social Worlds of Knowledge* (1949) he argued that a society's environment was coloured by the collective world outlook of its members,

> the environments to which societies are adjusted are worlds of ideas, collective representations that differ not only in extent and content, but also in structure.
> (1949a, 22)

Elsewhere he argued that the environment to which cultures adapted included both the internal and external social environment of the culture.

> In cultural adaptation the internal social environment is relatively more important than in biology. . . . A new

device, however 'efficient' from our standpoint, can be
adopted by a society only if it satisfies a socially approved
want and fits in to the whole cultural pattern. . . .

At the same time, the environment to which adaptation
is required includes other societies. A device or institution, however well adapted to the needs of a given society
and its physical environment, will be permanently beneficial only if it helps that society to adapt itself to its
neighbours. (1951a, 176)

It is interesting that during the thirties Childe regarded the
archaeologist's culture to be an observed fact, i.e. to be self-
evident on inspection of the archaeological record.

The culture is not an *a priori* category elaborated in the
studies of philosophers and then imposed from outside
upon working archaeologists. Cultures are observed facts.
The field worker does find specific types of tools, weapons,
and ornaments repeatedly associated together in graves
and habitations of one kind and contrasted with artefacts
found in graves and settlements of another kind.
(1935c, 3)

Later in his career however he was to become more aware of
the subjective element in the classification of cultures. As
archaeologists began to distinguish a multiplicity of cultures in
what had originally been viewed as single cultural groups, it
became clear that they were in fact exercising a choice in the
patterns which they perceived in the data.

Between the general discussion of culture in 'Changing
Methods and Aims' and the more detailed analysis of the
concept in the fifties, Childe's views on culture can only be
gleaned from brief passages in texts and papers concerned
with other subjects. For example in the introductory chapters
to two of his popular works, *Man Makes Himself* (1936) and
What Happened in History (1942) he devoted considerable
attention to the relationship between biological and cultural
evolution, using culture in the broad anthropological sense of
the term. It was only in the latter work, however, that he
explicitly discussed the idea of an archaeological culture.

Archaeologists classify the objects of their study not only
by function into knives, axes, huts, tombs and so on, but
also into different 'types' of knives, axes, dwellings and
graves. The several types of knife or tomb each fulfil
roughly the same function; the differences between them

repose upon divergences in the social tradition prescribing the methods of their preparation and use. In each functional class archaeologists can distinguish a variety of types current over a restricted area at a given period in archaeological time. The totality of recognised types current simultaneously in a given area is termed a 'culture'.
(1942a, 25, 26)

By now Childe was more cautious than in the thirties as to the nature of the sociological counterpart of the archaeologist's culture. Whereas previously he had attributed linguistic unity to the group now he warned that this was not necessarily the case.

It would be rash to try to define precisely what sort of social group corresponds to the archaeologist's 'culture'. Since language is such an important vehicle in the formation and transmission of social tradition, the group distinguished by the possession of a distinct 'culture' might be expected also to speak a distinct language. . . . Nevertheless culture and language need not coincide. The differences in equipment between Denmark, England, France and Germany are insignificant in comparison with the differences between Danish, English, French and German. (1942a, 26, 27)

As before, he emphasised the adaptive value of material culture, again stressing the biological analogy.

The human species is not physiologically adapted to any particular environment. Its adaptation is secured by its extracorporeal equipment of tools, clothes, houses and the rest . . . Material culture is thus largely a response to an environment.(1942a, 27, 28)

In the immediate post-war years Childe's brief discussions of the culture concept in works such as *Scotland Before the Scots*, published in 1946, serve to illustrate the fundamental continuity in his theoretical standpoint.

Prehistorians can distinguish two or more assemblages of relics and monuments that have divergent distributions in space but belong to the same stage or period. Technically, such contemporary or systadial assemblages are termed *cultures*. Prehistorians assume that each culture represents a distinct people or society; the peculiarities of its domestic architecture, burial ritual, ceramic decoration or fashions of ornament reflect the divergencies of the traditions that constitute the spiritual unity of each group. (1946a, 2)

By the late forties, however, there is a suggestion of a change in Childe's attitude to the definition of culture, for as the following passage shows he is beginning to question the useful-ness of the term in denoting the archaeologist's assemblage of associated traits.

> In any given archaeological period we find, often juxta-posed in a small area, different assemblages of tools, weapons, ornaments, house-types, burial rites and other archaeological traits repeatedly recurring together. Such recurrent assemblages we term – *rather unhappily* – *cul-tures*. We assume that each represents the durable part of the equipment or *culture* of an historical human society. Our assumption is just as well founded as is the palaeon-tologists' assumption that a fossil represents the harder part of an organism that was once clothed with flesh and lived. So archaeologists likewise try to reclothe with flesh their bare bones, to grasp their *so-called cultures* as the durable expressions of living and functioning organiza-tions of men. (1949a, 3, 4; my emphasis)

While Childe does not explicitly state the reasons for his change in attitude these can easily be inferred. By this time the concept of culture was widely employed in the social sciences as a whole to denote learned modes of behaviour, comprising both the material and non-material aspects of human society. The specialist sense peculiar to archaeology where culture is defined as a classificatory unit for material remains was thus significantly outwith the mainstream definition. If its usage in this sense was not explicitly stated, or if it were freely inter-changed with culture in the wider sense, as it had been in Childe's own work, ambiguities could arise.

By 1951 Childe felt it necessary to examine the relationship between the archaeological and anthropological view of cul-ture in some detail and in *Social Evolution* he devoted a whole chapter to the meaning of culture in both these senses. This was the first time that he had explicitly differentiated between the two usages. Basically he argued that the archaeologist's con-ception of a culture differed in degree rather than in kind from the anthropologist's. As before he defined an archaeological culture as 'an assemblage of associated traits that recur re-peatedly' (1951a, 30). Now he qualifies this statement, 'These

traits are mostly material objects,' (1951a, 30) thus by impli-
cation at least extending his definition of an archaeological
culture to comprise something other than material objects.

Culture in the anthropological sense he saw as basically a
holistic concept comprising all aspects of human behaviour that
are not innate reflexes or instincts.

> It is everything that men derive from nurture, from human
> society, rather than from nature or the sub-human en-
> vironment. It includes language and logic, religion and
> philosophy, morality and law, as well as the manufacture
> and use of tools, clothes, houses and even the selection of
> food to eat. All this men must learn from their fellows in
> society. The human infant has to learn from parents and
> seniors how to talk, how to dispose of his excrement, what
> to eat and how to prepare it, and so on. All these rules
> belong to the collective tradition, accumulated and pre-
> served by the society into which a human being is born.
> (1951a, 31, 32)

In addition to this holistic level Childe also recognised a
partitive level of culture, i.e. the acquired behaviour patterns
of particular groups. It was with this level that he equated the
archaeologist's culture.

> As societies have lived in different historical environments
> and have passed through different vicissitudes, their tradi-
> tions have diverged, and so ethnography reveals a multi-
> plicity of cultures, just as does archaeology. (1951a, 32)

In *Social Evolution* Childe argued that the social traditions
which determine culture are expressed in habits of thought and
action, in institutions and customs, all of which are essentially
immaterial and exist only so long as the society that inculcates,
sanctions and preserves them is alive and active. While writing
preserves language and with it clues to other non-material
aspects of past societies, the prehistorian does not have reference to this important source of material. For Childe, however,
this was not as great a problem as it might appear at first sight.

> For all culture finds expression in action – action in the
> material world. It is indeed through action alone that
> culture is maintained and transmitted; a belief that exists
> only in somebody's head forms no part of culture and has
> no existence for history or anthropology. Some of the
> actions dictated by, and expressive of, culture effect dur-
> able changes in the material world. All such fall within the

purview of archaeology. It is indeed just these human actions that have provided the material out of which archaeological cultures are constructed. (1951a, 33)

Childe thus emphasised that the archaeologist's knowledge of his cultures was not limited to a material level.

In a word, the archaeological record is by no means restricted to tools of production and weapons of war. Under suitable conditions we can learn a great deal about the mode of production as well as the means of production. The role of secondary and primary industry and of trade can be estimated from observed facts. The extent of the division of labour and the distribution of the product can be inferred with some confidence. Plausible guesses can be made as to the existence of slaves, the status of women, and the inheritance of property. Even the ideological superstructure can be made the subject of cautious hypotheses. (1951a, 34)

When Childe wrote *Social Evolution* he had been working with the idea of culture for over twenty-five years, also he had been deeply involved with both historical and philosophical theory. It was thus to be expected that his depth of understanding of both the limitations and potential of the concept would have increased. Even the briefest glance at the chapter shows that this is in fact the case. Whereas previously he had considered the archaeologist's culture to be an empirical entity immediately apparent on inspection of the archaeological record, now he was aware of a subjective element in the classification of data.

Culture and society are abstractions. No two products of handicraft are strictly identical. Every family of craftsmen and every member of such a family, have their own tricks of style. No two villages yield precisely the same complex of relics and traits. The subjective element comes in deciding which idiosyncracies should be ignored in defining a culture. Frankly, it is hard to say which should be disregarded as purely individual and which should be taken as social traits, the differentiae of new cultures. (1951a, 40)

At this time archaeologists were having to confront this problem directly since the broad cultural groupings which they had assumed to be unified wholes in the thirties were now seen to constitute several discrete groupings depending on the criterion selected as the classificatory basis. As noted previously when the cultural differentials became more refined, the number of cultures perceived in the archaeological record expended accordingly.

> German and Austrian archaeologists have been busily distinguishing new ceramic styles and making them the symbols, and often the eponyms, of new cultures. Plainly there must be limits to this subdivision. In England down to 1928, prehistorians recognised in their 'Early Bronze Age' a single culture, archaeologically symbolized by one type of pot, termed a 'Beaker', and identified with a single invading people, the 'Beaker-folk'. In 1948 at least four distinct kinds of Beaker have been distinguished and each attributed to different bands of invaders! (1951a, 40, 41)

However, while Childe recognised that the classification of cultures was not as objective as he had hitherto assumed, he did not discuss the matter in any depth and thus failed to emphasise its enormous implications for archaeological classification as a whole. The problem is in fact one of subjectivity and concerns the fundamental relationship between the archaeologist and his data. It is now widely recognised that the patterns perceived in the archaeological record are determined not only by the patterns inherent in the material itself, but also by the theoretical framework and taxonomic method of the archaeologist. Indeed Renfrew has recently suggested that the patterning of the archaeological record into cultural groups is to a great extent conditioned by the archaeologist's method of approach.

> It is easy to show how spatial distributions, equivalent to the traditional cultural entities, can be generated by the archaeologist out of a continuum of change. If uniformities and similarities in artefact assemblage are viewed as the result of interactions between individuals, and if such interactions decrease in intensity uniformly with distance, each point will be most like its close neighbours. Consider the point P lying in a uniform plane, with its neighbours fairly regularly spaced around it. Similarity in terms of trait c decreases with distance r from P. At the same time the variables A and B vary uniformly across the plane with distance along the axes x and y. If the excavator first digs at P and recovers its assemblage, he will subsequently learn that the adjacent points have a broadly similar assemblage, which he will call 'the P culture'. Gradually its boundaries will be set up by further research, with the

criterion that only those assemblages which attain a given threshold level of similarity with finds from P qualify for inclusion. So a 'culture' is born, centring on P, the type site, whose bounds are entirely arbitrary, depending solely on the threshold level of similarity and the initial fortuitous choice of P as the point of reference.

(Renfrew 1978, 94, 95)

The second area in which Childe's thinking had notably broadened since the thirties was in his appreciation of the nature of the sociological counterpart of the archaeologist's culture. By now he had realised that it did not necessarily correspond to either a linguistic grouping or a single society.

The boundaries of the several fields of culture do not necessarily coincide. The archaeologist has to rely mainly on material culture – instruments of production, transport devices, house plans, fashions of dress, artistic styles – in defining societies. Judged by these criteria, Europe, North America and Australia might easily seem to enjoy a single culture and therefore to represent a single society. But of course this relatively uniform cultural province is divided into several linguistic provinces, though language is a very important part of culture. It is split into a still larger number of economically and politically independent States, and many sociologists would identify State and society. At the same time each of these States is subdivided into smaller societies that may even cut across political boundaries – into churches and clubs, economic classes and professions and so on. The dress, housing, diet and even language of such groups within a single State often diverge very substantially. An archaeologist might take the material culture of each such group as representative of a distinct society. (1951a, 38)

Childe was thus very cautious as to what type of sociological grouping the archaeologist's culture corresponded to.

So for the archaeologist the unit or society must remain the group enjoying the same culture – i.e. giving concrete expression to common traditions. Such a group may comprise a number of settlements or local communities. Perhaps we might call its members a people, but we should have no right to assume that this people as a whole spoke a single language or acted as a political unit, still less that its members were related physiologically or belonged to one zoological race. (1951a, 40)

Recent work such as that of Clarke (1968) or Hodder (1978) have emphasised the complexity of the relationship between material culture and other aspects of society. At the same time it has been shown that the terms 'people' and 'tribe' are so vaguely defined by anthropologists that they encompass a wide range of social groups which vary greatly in complexity (Naroll 1964)

In view of this it has been convincingly argued by anthropologists and archaeologists alike that it is unimportant whether there is an exact correlation between archaeological and anthropological social groupings. Society may be classified in many different ways, according to a wide variety of models, and depending on the approach empoyed the social pattern selected will be different. In Clarke's words

> The archaeological culture maps a real entity that really existed, marking real interconnection – that this entity is not identical to historical, political, linguistic or racial entities does not make it less real or important. The archaeological entities reflect realities as important as those recognised by the traditional classifications of other disciplines; the entities in all these fields are equally real, equally arbitrary and simply different. (Clarke 1968, 364)

While Childe was clearly aware that cultural, linguistic and political parameters need not coincide, he was not as confident as Clarke in asserting the reality of the social counterpart of the archaeological culture as an alternative but equally valid grouping of society. Effectively, he hedged the problem by a subtle change in his usage of the term 'people'. Previously he had equated a 'culture' with a 'people' defined, however loosely, in essentially anthropological terms as a linguistic and social unit. In *Social Evolution*, while he retained the equation of a 'culture' with a 'people', it was only by redefining the latter term to the extent that its previous meaning was lost. In fact as the above passage shows (p. 63), it now denotes nothing more than the unit of society corresponding to the archaeological culture-group. What he has thus done is to change 'people' from an anthropological to an archaeological social unit, without however making this change fully explicit.

Childe was accustomed to devote a course of lectures every alternate year to 'the principles of archaeological classification, current terminology and implicit interpretative concepts'

(1956a, v). The outcome of this was *Piecing Together the Past* (1956), his most detailed statement of archaeological theory and methodology. In the same year he published *A Short Introduction to Archaeology*, which contained, in addition to chapters explaining the fundamentals of primitive technology and the main types of monuments found in the field, a precis of the theoretical argument advanced in *Piecing Together the Past*.

In both these works Childe's analysis was based on what he considered to be the three main co-ordinates in archaeological classification, functional, chronological and chorological. According to Childe these answered the questions 'What was it for?', 'When was it made?' and 'Who made it?' (1956a, 14–16; 1956b, 26–8). This tripartite basis, however, perhaps needs extending, for the third question 'Who made it?' in fact assumes and is based upon a more fundamental question. Strictly speaking since chorology is the scientific study of the geographical extents and limits of phenomena, the only question it can legitimately answer is 'Where is it found?' or 'What is its distribution?' The question of authorship is a distinct question which can only be considered after the functional, chronological and distributional factors have been determined. It is thus interesting that Childe saw only three rather than four basic co-ordinates. Presumably he considered the question of authorship to be so closely related to the question of distribution as not to require separate study.

For Childe a culture was fundamentally a chorological (spatial) and not a chronological unit. Cultural groupings he argued could not be used to denote periods of time but must themselves be classified chronologically. During Childe's lifetime this was an important and crucial point. At this time the key to the chronology of prehistoric Europe lay in the pattern of stratigraphically established culture sequences and it was thus normal practice to use cultural names to denote both geographical units of archaeological relics and monuments, and periods of relative chronology, i.e. that period during which a particular culture flourished.

In 1935 Childe had admitted that to a certain extent this practice was convenient, but even then he had warned that where there was the slightest danger of confusing the chronological with the cultural classification such usage was to be deprecated. At this time he suggested that if one wished to denote a period of time it was best done by using geological or climatological terms or dates in calendar years, thus removing the possibility of ambiguity.

Twenty years later in *Piecing Together the Past* he was even more firmly opposed to the practice of applying one and the same name to both a period and a culture, considering this to have been responsible for 'horrible confusion' (1956a, 95). Here he attempted to separate the chronological from the chorological co-ordinates by using a numerical system to denote the former and cultural terms for the latter.

Childe however was not wholly enthusiastic about the system and expressed several reservations as to its practical application. First, he pointed out that there was a real danger that bizarre cultural terms might be replaced by equally bizarre numerical terms.

> But even in the well-explored provinces of the British Isles, northern Europe and Greece, recent surprises have warned us that familiar and well-recognised cultural sequences may be susceptible of extension and subdivision. Allowance for such refinement can be made by using Roman numerals for the major periods already recognised. Divisions in each could then be denoted by letters and subdivisions by Arabic figures, so we might have III B 1 (or even III B 1 c using a lower case letter for further subdivisions!). (1956a, 100)

Secondly he emphasised that numerical designations had only a limited regional validity; for example in Britain despite its relatively small size, there was no system that could be applied to the province as a whole (1956a, 101).

Childe's concept of an archaeological culture was based on the notion of an archaeological type, which he considered to be the smallest unit of archaeological classification. Essentially a type was an abstraction, a grouping together of phenomena. He emphasised that the archaeologist was not interested in unique objects but rather in those which had been accepted and replicated by society. Indeed it was this very replication which, in Childe's eyes, constituted the essence of the type. 'Types are just creations of individuals that have been approved, adopted and objectified by some society' (1956a, 9). The prehistorian thus, according to Childe, only deals with the individual as a member of a class, ignoring what he termed 'the particular peculiarities, accidental or intentional, that in fact distinguish

each specimen' (1956a, 6). This is of course where the personal
viewpoint of the archaeologist is of crucial importance for how
does one decide which traits are to be selected and which are to
be rejected. As pointed out previously Childe was aware of and
alluded to a subjective element in archaeological classification.
In *Piecing Together the Past*, he again raised this issue.

> Finally, how precisely should types be defined for choro-
> logical – and for that matter for chronological – classifi-
> cation? No two handmade articles are identical. All types
> are abstractions obtained by ignoring the minor deviations
> of individual specimens.

> Archaeologists have in practice proceeded not by
> grouping together ever wider assemblages of increasingly
> abstract types, but rather by subdividing such groups by
> discriminating even more concrete types. How far can
> such discrimination profitably procede? (1956a, 124)

Here he argued that no general rules could be laid down *a priori*
and while he offered a few practical hints on how to proceed in
two concrete instances, he was largely content to leave the
solution of the problem to the archaeologist's own discretion.

When types are signiificantly associated, i.e. in a context
which indicates contemporary use, the notion of culture arises.
Here Childe emphasised that simple juxtaposition does not
necessarily imply association for this might be the result of
chance. In such instances he advocated the use of Braidwood's
term 'aggregate'.

> When a group of types are found together under circum-
> stances suggesting contemporary use they are said to be
> *associated*. Mere physical juxtaposition does not guaran-
> tee association. A number of stone implements may turn
> up together in a gravel pit dug in a Pleistocene river
> channel. The gravel consists of debris picked up by the
> river and its tributaries anywhere in its large catchment
> area and promiscuously dumped together where the force
> of the current abated. There is no guarantee that all the
> implements included in the gravel had been made or used
> together or even in the same geological period; some
> might have been washed out of older gravels laid down
> millennia earlier and then mixed with others made and
> used on the surface of those older gravels. Braidwood
> describes such a fortuitous collection as an *aggregate*.
> (1956a, 31)

He made the further provision that cultures must illustrate more than one aspect of human behaviour, for example a recurrent assemblage of stone tools never found in any recognisable type of dwelling or grave or even associated with broken bones of game indicative of a selection of menus, he termed an 'industry', not a culture (1956a, 33). When cultures were seen to be what he termed 'genetically' related to a mother culture, and collaterally to one another, as he believed the Danubian cultures to be, these constituted a 'culture-cycle'.

> The totality of genetically related cultures constitutes the simplest case of what I propose to designate a *cycle* (of cultures) or culture-cycle. A more objective definition would be: All cultures, characterized by the same families of types, belong to the same cycle. If then the habitat of a culture be termed a *province*, let us say that cycles occupy *spheres*. (1956a, 142)

Childe, then, proposed an archaeological hierarchy of type, industry, culture and culture-cycle, a hierarchy which was to be rationalised and interpreted in terms of systems theory by D. Clarke (1968) in the late sixties.

In *Piecing Together the Past* as in *Social Evolution* Childe drew attention to the fact that archaeologists were beginning to discern an ever increasing number of cultural groupings in their data, often distinguished on the basis of quite fine criteria. This of course was a major blow to his earlier thesis that cultures are observed facts. In effect it meant that he had not only to look more carefully at the nature of these groupings but to examine in more detail the way in which they were differentiated. For Childe this necessitated a close look at the geologically inspired concept of a type-fossil. Here he emphasised that type-fossils were often constituted by very insignificant aspects of behaviour.

> To distinguish one culture from another, the most convenient differentiae, the most serviceable diagnostic fossils are offered by the more superficial, often indeed trivial, idiosyncracies of behaviour – traits that are least obviously integrated with the total pattern. (1956a, 113)

Many other types indicative of highly significant cultural behaviour were of little value for diagnostic purposes because they occur over vast areas of time and space. While they are essential for describing cultures they are unsuitable for differentiating them (1956a, 33). In order to determine the significance of a proposed type-fossil as a cultural differential Childe believed that the subjective element could be largely overcome by reference to distributional analysis. Here he argued that if a type were truly diagnostic of a culture, its distribution should exhibit an intelligible pattern clustered around one or more recognisable foci.

> The standard distributional pattern for a relic that is a good diagnostic type will be a nucleus of thick set dots surrounded by a penumbra, or several such nuclei.
> (1956a, 116)

It is interesting to compare this model with that proposed in the 1939 edition of *The Dawn*, where Childe advocated a similar pattern against which to test his short chronology for prehistoric Europe. In neither case did he attempt to verify the model or even indicate the evidence upon which it is based. The existence of a primary centre of diffusion and the pattern of diffusion therefrom, however, cannot be taken as axiomatic but rather as a hypothesis requiring verification. That Childe did not see this, especially in a work explicitly devoted to archaeological theory, is thus significant for it illustrates an important blindspot in his approach where he is so strongly influenced by the diffusionist paradigm as to lose sight of the hypothetical nature of its fundamental premises. It must be admitted then that Childe's attempt to evaluate the diagnostic potential of type-fossils was unsuccessful.

Here it might be noted that it is precisely this culture-centre hypothesis which sustains what Binford has termed the 'normative' explanation of cultural variation.

> Cultural differences and similarities are expressed by the normative school in terms of 'cultural relationships' which, if treated rigorously, resolve into one general interpretative model. This model is based on the assumption of a 'culture center' where, for unspecified reasons, rates of innovation exceed those in surrounding areas. The new culture spreads out from the center and blends with surrounding cultures until it is dissipated at the fringes, leaving marginal cultures. (Binford 1972b, 126)

Childe stressed that a culture should not be distinguished by a single type but by a plurality of well-defined diagnostic types thus avoiding any unnecessary proliferation of cultural groups. However, while he admitted that a quantitative element entered into the definition of culture he argued that statistics could only have a limited use in the discipline.

> We say that a type to be diagnostic of a culture must 'normally' have been found associated with other diagnostic types. And 'normally' presumably means '*n* times'. Yet it is impracticable to fix a precise numerical value for *n*. Carved stone balls were once found in association with other types distinctive of the Rinyo culture. In the absence of any other association for these curious objects, we have to assume that the remaining one hundred and twenty balls found in isolation belonged to the Rinyo culture and can be used to illustrate its one time distribution.

> Of course a few stray specimens of a diagnostic type far from the region of its main concentration do not suffice to prove the spread thither of the culture they should typify. But laborious statistical calculations are hardly necessary to unmask the spurious chronological claims of such strays. (1956a, 122, 123)

Childe's approach to the differentiation of cultural groups was thus essentially a qualitative one based on presence or absence of type-fossils. In the light of modern quantitative methodology based on computer technology, it can now be seen as a relatively crude classificatory tool which not only obscures information but greatly oversimplifies the spatial patterns existing in the archaeological record (Shennan 1978).

Childe emphasised at several points throughout the text that the archaeologist's culture was not constituted by type-fossils, they merely provided the framework for further study.

> The substance of the record is constituted by the houses of the living and the dead with the evidence of daily activities and the solemn rituals they supply, the craftsmen's tools through which the practical science of past ages was applied, the carvings or paintings that directly express ideas and ideals. If their arrangement and classification depend upon the most variable and improbable playthings of fashion, that does not exempt or preclude the archaeologist from studying and presenting the permanent contributions made by the age and by the society that in each case is defined by its most ephemeral fancies. (1956a, 38)

Once a cultural grouping had been distinguished in the archaeological record with the aid of diagnostic types, Childe argued that the next step was to enumerate all types and phenomena associated with them, thus providing the basis for inference concerning the behaviour of the group. Here Childe divided a culture into three main sections, each comprising several subsections.

ECONOMY
I Primary economy
   (a) Habitat. (b) Food supply.
   (c) Warmth and shelter.
II Industries
   (a) Stoneworking. (b) Metallurgy. (c) Bone, horn and ivory. (d) Carpentry. (e) Pottery. (f) Textiles and basketry. (g) Hides. (h) Other natural materials.
III Transport
   (a) By water. (b) By land.
IV Trade
V War

SOCIOLOGY
I Demography
II Family as an institution
III Town planning
IV Structure

IDEOLOGY
I Scientific
   (a) Writing and numerical notation. (b) Counting.
   (c) Measurement. (d) Geometry. (e) Calendrical science. (f) Medicine and surgery.
II Numenological
   (a) Burial rites. (b) 1. temples and sanctuaries; 2. figurines, idols and phalli; 3. aniconic ritual objects.
   (c) Rites.
III Artistic
   (a) Graphic arts. (b) Musical instruments.
   (c) Personal ornaments.
IV Sportive
   (a) Knuckle bones, dice, draughtsmen. (b) Cursus and ball-courts. (c) Toys and rattles.
   (1956a, 129-31)

As in 1935 Childe stressed that culture should be viewed as an organic whole and not as a mechanical aggregate of traits (1956a, 34). It is thus perhaps somewhat surprising that he

71

does not accompany his detailed compilation of the contents of culture with a discussion as to how the major subdivisions inter-relate within the whole.

In fact the only place where he even briefly considers this problem is in a chapter entitled 'What is it for?' but here he is only concerned with the inter-relationship between what he terms spiritual and material culture. As before he defines the latter in a specialist utilitarian sense.

> The bulk of the archaeological record falls within the domain, tritely termed 'Material Culture'. Most archaeo-logical data, that is to say, result from actions directed towards the satisfaction of needs that *Homo Sapiens* shares with other animals. Of course such satisfaction is in all cases sought or obtained in a distinctively human way and in particular with the aid of extra corporeal organs – artefacts, not organically attached to the human body nor yet produced from it like a spider's web. With this qualifi-cation it may be said that at least a large proportion of our relics and monuments served, albeit only very indirectly and in a roundabout way, to the procurement of food, shelter, warmth, protection against foes human and non human, and hygiene. (1956a, 44, 45)

While he did not define 'spiritual culture' he gave examples as to what is to be included in this class.

> For descriptive purposes the monuments and relics resul-ting from . . . ritual, sportive or artistic activities may be relegated to the category of 'Spiritual Culture'.
> (1956a, 44)

His main point was that since no society could indulge in ceremonies, games and ornaments, unless it produced enough food and shelter to support itself, the 'spiritual culture' could legitimately be called a superstructure supported by the pro-ductive system (1956a, 44)

The fact that Childe did not discuss the theory underlying his tripartite division of the archaeological culture relegated what might have been an exposition of a system with interrelated subsystems to a catalogue of material items which in his own words had no claims to being 'exhaustive or even logical' (1956a, 128)

At the same time his reluctance to explicate the anthropo-logical theory of culture, which throughout his career had implicitly supported his own archaeological definition, left him with a purely taxonomic unit of dubious value. In the thirties he had extolled the virtues of this unit in that he believed it to have arisen naturally from the archaeological record. Twenty years later the differentiation of these 'natural packages' was seen to involve a number of serious taxonomic problems which archaeological methodology at that time was simply not equipped to deal with.

This is not to undervalue Childe's contribution to the development of the culture concept in archaeology. Viewed against the 'normative' framework of his contemporaries Childe's views were certainly advanced and in many respects anticipated further developments in the sixties and seventies. Unlike 'normative' theorists, he did not see his field of study as 'the ideational basis of the varying ways of human life' (Binford 1972b, 26). In fact on several occasions Childe made it clear that he saw the reconstruction of the past thoughts of prehistoric man to be a futile exercise based on a false understanding of the nature of knowledge (1949a, 1956a, 171–2). This is discussed more fully in chapter 5.

Secondly unlike 'normative' theorists Childe did not view culture as a vast whole but rather in terms of three different subsections, i.e. economy, sociology and ideology. (Compare with Binford's (1972a) technomic, sociotechnic and ideotechnic categories.) In this context it should also be noted that Childe was aware of what Clarke (1968) has termed the polythetic nature of culture, i.e. that boundaries of the several sub-sections do not necessarily correlate. Finally, like new theorists such as Binford, Childe saw culture in terms of adaptation to an environment which like the latter he defined in social as well as geophysical terms. Childe, however, did not view adaptation as a necessary function of all cultural components and thus avoided the circularities of the modern definitions (Burnham 1973).

3

The Functional–Economic Interpretation
of the Three Ages

At the same time as he introduced his functional conception of culture to the Prehistoric Society in 1935, Childe also presented what he termed his functional-economic interpretation of the three-age model of Stone, Bronze and Iron. Before going on to discuss this interpretation, however, it is essential to outline the development of the model prior to 1935, for unlike the cultural paradigm the three-age model had a relatively long history in the discipline and had undergone several fundamental changes in the course of its evolution (Heizer 1962, Daniel 1943, 1967).

In 1836 Christian Jurgensen Thomsen published *Ledetraad til Nordisk Old Kyndighed* which was translated into English in 1848 as *A Guide to Northern Antiquities* by Lord Ellesmere. This contained what was undoubtedly the most explicit and detailed statement of the idea of three ages of Stone, Bronze and Iron to date.

> *The Age of Stone*, or that period when weapons and implements were made of stone, wood or bone, or some such material, and during which very little or nothing at all was known of metals. . . .
> *The Age of Bronze*, in which weapons and cutting implements were made of copper or bronze, and nothing at all, or but very little was known of iron or silver. . . .
> *The Age of Iron* is the third and last period of the heathen times, in which iron was used for those articles to which that metal is eminently suited, and in the fabrication of which it came to be used as a substitute for bronze.
> (Thomsen in Daniel 1967, 93–5)

The simplicity of Thomsen's technological model, however, was not to endure long. With the discovery of the antiquity of man and of manufactured tools associated with the bones of extinct animals, important structural changes had to be made in order to accommodate the long duration of the first age. In 1865 Lubbock divided the Stone Age into two major periods, the Palaeolithic and the Neolithic.

    i. That of the Drift; when man shared possession of Europe with the Mammoth, the Cave Bear, the Woolly-haired Rhinoceros and other extinct animals. This I have proposed to call the 'Palaeolithic' Period.

    ii. The later or polished Stone Age; a period characterised by beautiful weapons and instruments made of flint and other kinds of stone; in which, however, we find no trace of the knowledge of any metal, excepting gold, which seems to have been sometimes used for ornaments. For this period I have suggested the term 'Neolithic'.

(Lubbock in Daniel 1967, 120)

He thus introduced new geological and ecological criteria into what had been hitherto a purely technological scheme.

By the end of the nineteenth century it was shown that these three sets of criteria did not coincide. To accommodate a period which was geologically recent and had chipped stone implements the term Mesolithic was suggested by Allen Brown (1892), but Boyd Dawkins (1894) disapproved of the suggestion and the term was not generally accepted until the nineteen-twenties.

European archaeologists working on the Bronze Age in the last thirty years of the nineteenth century were likewise seeing major divisions in their material. Italian archaeologists, for example Pigorini, Collini and Orsi, proposed an 'Eneolithic Period' between the end of the Stone Age and the beginning of the Bronze Age. In Hungary at the International Congress at Budapest in 1876, François Von Pulszky proposed the recognition of a Copper Age between the Stone Age and the Bronze Age. Sir William Wilde in his *Catalogue of the Antiquities in the Museum of the Royal Irish Academy* in 1863 likewise distinguished between a copper and bronze industry. French archaeologists were also beginning to recognise a copper stage prior to the Bronze Age. In 1865 Jeanjean in his *L'Age du Cuivre dans les Cévennes* argued for a copper age in the south of France calling it Durfortian after the Grotte des Morts at Durfort. The researches of Saint Venant, Raymond and Chatellier in Brittany seemed to confirm the existence of this Copper Age. Chantre in 1875/76 in his *L'Age du Bronze* regarded the Bronze Age as a unitary phase preceded by the Copper Age.

The Iron Age at this time did not undergo any major alterations as far as its meaning or implications were concerned. It was realised, however, that throughout the greater part of historic time in Western Europe man had been using iron, so the term early or pre-Roman Iron Age was usually employed to specify the initial phase.

During the nineteenth century the three-age model served as the basis for an elaborate chronological structuring of archaeological data from prehistoric Europe. Thus as well as advocating additional ages, archaeologists at this time began to seriate the ages themselves. Undoubtedly the most influential subdivision of the Stone Age was that by Gabriel de Mortillet in 1869 and 1872, in which he recognised four major periods in the Palaeolithic: (1) Epoque du Moustier; (2) Epoque du Solutré; (3) Epoque d'Aurignac; and (4) Epoque de la Madeleine. In 1872 in his paper at the International Congress at Brussels he dropped the Epoque d'Aurignac and divided the Palaeolithic into two major divisions; a Lower, containing Chellean, Mousterian and Solutrean, and an Upper consisting of Magdalenian. He also hoped to bring the Neolithic into line by terming it Robenhousien after the Swiss site of Robenhausen.

De Mortillet's system was basically an extension of the principles of geology applied to archaeology. In his *Préhistorique* (1883) he wrote

> Suivant d'une excellente méthode adoptée en géologie – il ne faut pas oublier que la paléoethnologie découle directement de la géologie – j'ai donné à chaque époque le nom d'une localité bien typique, parfaitement connue et étudiée; seulement, au lieu de dire: époque de Chelles, époque du Moustier, époque du Solutre et époque de la Madeleine; pour simplifier, en supprimant l'article, j'ai transformé en adjectif le nom de la localité, le terminant par d'une consonance uniforme. C'est encore là un procédé emprunté à la géologie.
>
> (De Mortillet in Daniel 1975, 108)

Thus although his classification was based on sites, the subdivisions represented not cultures but periods of time deduced from techno-typological criteria. To a certain extent this tradition of subdividing the ages was carried on into the Bronze and Iron Ages by Montelius and others. Montelius's scheme for the Bronze Age was developed in three famous works; *Les Temps Préhistoriques en Suede et dans les autres Pays Scandi-*

naves (1895), *La Civilisation Primitive en Italie depuis l'Intro-duction des Métaux* (1895) and *Die Chronologie der ältesten Bronzezeit en Nord-Deutschland und Scandinavien* (1900). In northern Europe Montelius recognised five phases which he numbered i–v, in Italy he identified only i–iv with a subdivision in phase i. Montelius's use of numbers to distinguish postulated periods was a significant departure from the French-named epochs and formed the basis for the numerical chronologies of the pre-radiocarbon dated schemes of the twentieth century, in particular those of Childe.

Similar schemes were devised during the last quarter of the nineteenth century for subdividing the Iron Age. In 1872 Hildebrand distinguished the Halstatt and La Tène phases in the pre-Roman Iron Age. In 1875 de Mortillet adopted this dual division but termed the second phase Gaulish or Marnian Iron Age. In 1885 Otto Tischler divided La Tène into three periods on a typological basis.

During the nineteenth century, then, the major theoretical influence on the three-age model came from contemporary geology. The Ages and their subdivisions were thus viewed as 'epochs' and considered to represent units of sidereal time. By the turn of the century, however, the practical demonstration of the contemporaneity of many of the alleged epochs led archaeologists to look more closely at the nature of their basic units. And with the recognition that the variation in the archaeological record could be explained by changes in social tradition as well as changes in time, the concept of culture began to replace the epoch as the primary unit of classification. However, while this necessitated changes in the intricate substructure of the three-age model it did not seriously affect its overall role in the discipline.

It was only during the course of the twentieth century, with the expansion of archaeological research from a European to a global basis, that the usefulness of the major divisions as chronological periods came to be questioned. In this wider context it became apparent that the model had only a very limited field of application and could in fact be only usefully employed in the Old World, in particular Northern Europe. In America, Africa or Australia the existence of 'Stone Age' or 'Iron Age' peoples side by side with modern civilisation highlighted its basic weakness as a chronological framework. Childe, himself, it should be noted, was among the first to point out the inadequacies of the model in this respect.

Geological periods have an absolute value and are applicable equally to all continents and latitudes only because they are so enormously long that temporal differences between events in distinct areas are relatively insignificant. Natural history must take these periods as units. The fossil flora or fauna characteristic of a geological period did not presumably appear simultaneously all over the world, but originated in one centre from which it slowly spread. But with the geological period, defined by the fossils, as unit, the time occupied by the spread is imperceptible. With his limitations and for his purposes the palaeontologist must ignore time lags between regions, for him all *Edaphosauri* are 'contemporary'.

The prehistorian of humanity cannot afford to make abstraction of such lags. Judged by their industries the New Zealand Maoris in the days of Captain Cook and the Tasians of the Nile Valley before 5000 B.C. were both 'neolithic'. Polished stone axes treated as *Leitfossilen* would make the Maoris of the 18th century A.D. contemporaries of the Egyptians who nevertheless lived sixty centuries earlier in terms of human history! A period which telescopes into nothingness the whole of written history is useless as a chronological frame for prehistory.

Typological periods can have at best a regional validity, can provide a convenient but provisional framework for classifying local antiquities. Thomsen's three ages did enable him to arrange his collection of Danish relics in the right chronological order. It would have broken down had it been extended to collections from Greece and Greenland. To determine what Danish products should be displayed as contemporary with Bronze Age relics from Greece or Esquimaux Stone Age artefacts a time scale quite independent of the material must be invoked. (1935c, 2)

However, while he rejected the three ages as a chronological framework, he did not believe that the model had outlived its role in the discipline. By a revolutionary shift in emphasis he suggested that it could provide a useful framework for socio-economic development.

What then is to become of the hallowed terms, Palaeolithic, Neolithic, Bronze Age and Iron Age? Can they survive as designations of true periods of time which could be expressed in terms of solar years in our calendar? Obviously not. But I should like to believe they can be given a profound significance as indicating vital stages in human progress? (1935c, 7)

Elsewhere he made it clear that he considered the criteria selected by Thomsen, i.e. the material used for the principal cutting tools and weapons, to be meaningful indices of economic and social systems.

The archaeologist's division of the prehistoric period into Stone, Bronze and Iron Ages are not altogether arbitrary. They are based upon the materials used for cutting implements, especially axes, and such implements are among the most important tools of production. Realist history insists upon their significance in moulding and determining social systems and economic organization. (1936a, 9)

These criteria are no superficial symptoms, but organically bound up with the economy and structure of the societies to be classified. After all, cutting tools constitute, at least in the less well-equipped societies, a decisive part of the means of production at the disposal of those societies. In fact, a comparative study of societies classified on this basis brings out very prettily the influence of the *means* of production on the *mode* of production. (1946c, 18–19)

Thus Childe believed that with the aid of a Marxist model of history he could interpret the three ages of Stone, Bronze and Iron in socio-economic terms. However, before going on to examine the economic and sociological values which he gave to the ages, it is essential to consider the classificatory basis of the interpretation. For while Childe stressed the advantages of a model based on technological criteria, the three-age system at this time was no longer purely technological in basis but during the course of its development had acquired in a non-systematic fashion other classificatory criteria. This was most evident in the context of the Neolithic which by this time was characterised by a whole set of diverse criteria, i.e. by polished stone axes, by pottery and agriculture as well as by a geological age – the holocene.

In 'Changing Methods and Aims in Prehistory' Childe retained Thomsen's original technological criteria for the Bronze and Iron Ages, i.e. the material used for the principal cutting tools and weapons, while emphasising economic criteria for the subdivisions of the Stone Age. 'Neolithic will mean "food producing" and will point a contrast with the food-gathering economy of the Old Stone Age' (1935c, 7). While he argued that this definition of the Neolithic agreed passably with classical definitions, he had in fact to reject the polished stone axe as a criterion of Neolithic culture.

> The polished stone axe that marks the neolithic period of the typologist was and is used by food-gatherers. The great comb-ware culture of north-eastern Europe exhibits the typologically neolithic traits of polished stone and pottery, but its economic foundation was food-gathering; its economy is palaeolithic though its industry is formally neolithic. Conversely a typical group of self-sufficing food producers like the Badarians apparently used no polished stone axes; presumably they had no use for them, since timber was scarce or non-existent. A polished stone axe is not, therefore, a conclusive or necessary sign of a neolithic culture. (1935c, 8)

Furthermore as the following passage shows he was not wholly convinced as to the usefulness of pottery as an index of the Neolithic.

> But pottery used to be regarded as exclusively neolithic. Yet Dr. Leakey found sherds in a pleistocene deposit in Kenya. And recently Burchell and Reid Moir have eloquently restated the case for palaeolithic pottery in Europe too. Their arguments and others have convinced me that palaeolithic pottery is a possibility to be reckoned with. (1935c, 8)

At this time, however, Childe was not completely wholehearted in his rejection of the technological criteria and gave a separate status to those cultures which he regarded as 'formally neolithic' while based on a hunting-gathering economy.

> Some term like opsipalaeolithic or opsimiolithic ought to be adopted to describe cultures which are formally neolithic or contemporary with neolithic cultures, but still preserve the food gathering economy of the Old Stone Age. (1935c, 8)

It is interesting that at this point Childe tentatively retained the equation between the Palaeolithic and the Pleistocene, suggesting that if 'the cultivation of plants in the upper pleistocene could be established the significance attached to the terms palaeolithic or neolithic would have to be changed' (1935c, 8). Elsewhere he writes,

> The Old Stone Age was indeed so enormously long that it may be treated as a universal period, equivalent to the geologists' pleistocene. But in considering its end the time lag between the different areas is of crucial importance. The equivalence between pleistocene and palaeolithic is preserved by many archaeologists through the insertion of a Mesolithic Age, to which are assigned some post-glacial archaeological remains from countries, like Britain and North-Western Europe in general, which were only affected by the neolithic revolution long after the end of the Ice Age. To the mesolithic would then be assigned those remains that are later than the geological pleistocene but older than the beginnings of the New Stone Age locally. (1936a, 50)

Later in his career, however, Childe was to become more critical of this equation, considering it to have arisen from a lack of understanding of the difference between absolute and relative chronology. In this context he was firmly opposed to the introduction of the concept of Mesolithic into the model, believing it to have caused further confusion.

> This innovation can only be regarded as deplorable. For it sanctioned and stereotyped a confusion foreign to the founders of the Three Age system. Thomsen had to arrange the prehistoric material from a small and homogeneous area. In Denmark Stone, Bronze and Iron described real Ages – periods of time which followed one another in that order. Because the same sequence was observed in other parts of Europe and eventually in Egypt and Hither Asia it did not follow that the several 'Ages' were everywhere contemporary. Thomsen probably never envisaged this possibility. His immediate successors, like Worsaae explicitly denied it; the Bronze Age began in Egypt and the Eastern Mediterranean much earlier than in the North.
>
> But with Lubbock's division of the Stone Age, one half of it had been identified with a geological period, the Pleistocene. (1951a, 19–20)

Throughout his career Childe consistently advocated an economic basis of classification for the subdivisions of the Stone

Age, while retaining the technological criteria for the major ages. In other words he employed an essentially mixed model of the past. In *Piecing Together the Past* (1956) he defended such practice, arguing that it was quite logical to introduce a new basis of classification for the subdivisions (1956a, 86). The situation is complicated, however, by the fact that while Childe thus characterised the Palaeolithic and Neolithic as subdivisions of the Stone Age, in his initial functional-economic interpretation he seemed to give the Palaeolithic, Neolithic, Bronze and Iron Ages equal status as economic stages. This identity of status was emphasised by the fact that the Neolithic, Bronze and Iron Ages were all preceded by economic revolutions.

Childe retained this four-fold structure until very late in his career when he replaced it by a five-fold division. In *Piecing Together the Past* he argued that the lower and middle Palaeolithic represented a technological grouping which was separate and distinct from the upper Palaeolithic/Mesolithic assemblages. Childe termed the first subdivision of the Stone Age the Protolithic or Palaeolithic and the second subdivision the Miolithic (1956a, 86). The Neolithic was retained as the third subdivision but unlike the Protolithic and the Miolithic it was defined by economic criteria, i.e. food production (1956a, 87). The Bronze and Iron Ages were defined traditionally by the material used for the principal cutting tools and weapons (1956a, 89–90).

Daniel, in his critique of the three ages in 1943, argued that Childe had in fact introduced a new and alternative model of prehistory which did not coincide with Thomsen's three ages. In his eyes they were two 'separate and different groupings of human history – the one technological, the other functional-economic' (Daniel 1943, 48). Certainly, Childe's reinterpretation of the three ages suggests a separate economic model. Childe, however, never attempted to give it a distinct status outside the three-age framework. During his lifetime archaeological research was not geared to gaining direct access to economic facts. Rather these had to be inferred from the technology. Even in 1956 Childe drew attention to this in the context of the neolithic.

> In practice the criterion is not so readily applicable; from a few bones it is not easy to distinguish domesticated from wild animals; actual remains of vegetable foods are only in exceptional circumstances preserved. Hence all evidence

for farming might be missing unless farmers made specialized and easily recognisable implements for reaping or
grinding grain – and there are no reasons for suspecting
that the very earliest farmers did.

Prehistorians once hoped to dodge this practical difficulty, believing that all farmers manufactured pots and
most at least polished stone for axe-blades. Since 1950,
however, it has been demonstrated that the earliest farmers in Palestine, Cyprus, Kurdistan and Baluchistan did
not make pots, while at least in Palestine they made no
recognisable axes at all and certainly made none with
polished edges. (1956a, 87–8)

Practical reasons aside, however, it is clear that Childe believed that Thomsen's ages coincided with major stages in
man's socio-economic development. As indicated above,
Childe held a Marxist view of society in which a particular level
of technology was seen to correspond to a definite form of
economy and sociology. In terms of this model, the stone,
bronze and iron technologies should be indicative of economic
and social systems suited to the specific demands of each technology.

The Stone Age

Childe made two major points concerning Stone Age economy, first that it was self-sufficient and secondly that it lacked
full-time specialisation. Interestingly, he saw these traits as
characteristic of both Palaeolithic and Neolithic stages, although the latter represented a food-producing and the former
a food-gathering economy (1935c, 7; 1936a, 54–117; 1954b,
40–4). While Childe was aware that trade was carried out
during the Stone Age he believed that it was confined to
luxuries.

Trade in the sense of transmission of commodities from
one group to another is indeed quite well attested in the
Stone Age, even in the Old Stone Age. But the objects of
Stone Age trade were always luxuries – if not merely shells
or similar 'ornaments' at least things that men could easily
have done without. A Stone Age community was, at least
potentially, self-sufficing. (1951a, 25–6)

Childe assumed that metal was the first indispensable article
of commerce as contrasted with luxuries which at a pinch
societies could do without. In this context he argued that two

factors contributed to the conversion of metal from a luxury into a necessity.

> On the one hand, under the peculiar conditions of the alluvial valleys like the Tigris-Euphrates delta, where even stone is scarce, the greater durability of copper or bronze tools may have made them actually more economical than stone or obsidian. On the other hand, in war, especially for in-fighting, a copper dagger or knife is much more reliable than a flint one; the latter may break just at the awkward moment when you must stab your enemy or perish. (1942a, 71)

When Childe discussed the social structure of the Stone Age he made no attempt to assess any changes in society which might have occurred as a result of the food-producing revolution. Basically, he argued that during the Stone Age, society was organised along kinship lines – a type of structuring which like Durkheim he saw as 'mechanical' as opposed to 'organic'.

> Community of employment, the common absorption in obtaining food by similar devices, guarantees a certain solidarity to the group. For co-operation is essential to secure food and shelter and for defence against foes, human and subhuman. This identity of economic interests and pursuits is echoed and magnified by identity of language, custom and belief; rigid conformity is enforced as effectively as industry in the common quest for food. But conformity and industrious co-operation need no State organization to maintain them. The local group usually consists either of the single clan . . . or a group of clans related by habitual intermarriage. And the sentiment of kinship is reinforced or supplemented by common rites focused on some ancestral shrine or sacred place. Archaeology can provide no evidence for kinship organization, but shrines occupied the central place in preliterate villages in Mesopotamia, and the long barrow, a collective tomb that overlooks the presumed site of most neolithic villages in Britain, may well have been also the ancestral shrine on which converged the emotions and ceremonial activities of the villagers below. However, the solidarity thus idealized and concretely symbolized, is really based on the same principles as that of a pack of wolves or a herd of sheep; Durkheim has called it 'mechanical'. (1950e, 7)

At the same time he argued that this type of society was

potentially an example of what Marxists termed 'primitive communism'.

> The means of production of the Stone Stage are not incompatible with 'primitive communism' if that means the collective ownership of gardens, flocks and herds and such instruments of production as are jointly used, like fishing nets. (1946c, 20)

The Bronze Age

In 1930 Childe published *The Bronze Age*, a work in which he attempted to rehabilitate Thomsen's second age as a major stage in economic as well as technological development. Here he argued that the invention of bronze metallurgy was a major advance in the history of science implying a knowledge of the radical transformation of the physical properties of substance by heat. Secondly, he emphasised that the general use of metal presupposes regular and extensive trade relations. Each farmer must sacrifice his self-sufficiency in order to purchase metal tools from experts.

> At the same time, within a given ethnic group, the individual farmer must sacrifice his economic independence and the village its self-sufficiency as the price of the new material. Each Neolithic household could and did manufacture the requisite knives, axe-heads and awls of flint, stone or bone; the Neolithic village need never look beyond its own domains for the necessary material – nor did, save in the case of luxury articles such as shells. But metal tools the farmer must . . . purchase from the expert, the village smith. And the latter must, except in exceptional circumstances, import his raw materials from outside the communal boundaries. This is perhaps the essential difference between the Neolithic and the Bronze Ages. (1930a, 8–9)

Thus as early as 1930 we find that Childe's basic argument concerning the essential characteristics of the Bronze Age is already formed. As the following passages show he was to uphold the main points in this argument throughout his career. In 1935 when he introduced his functional-economic interpretation of the three ages he writes

> The regular use of metal generally broke down this independence and self-sufficiency. The smith, like the miner, is a specialized craftsman; his materials, the metals or their

ores, have nearly always to be obtained from other regions or peoples by some more or less regular system of trade or barter.

The use of copper and still more of bronze is thus the symptom of a radical change in economic structure in the direction of modern conditions. It indicates specialization of labour and the beginnings of regular foreign trade. (1935c, 7–80)

And in 1951,

In the first place it marks, perhaps, the beginning of specialization of labour – what Engels more accurately designates 'the separation of handicraft from agriculture'. . . . On ethnographic evidence smiths are generally full-time specialists; they neither grow nor catch their own food, but get it in return for the products of their craft. As far as archaeological evidence can go, this applies to prehistoric bronze-smiths. They are the first full-time specialists attested in human history.

Secondly the regular use of copper or bronze was possible only in so far as regular trade was organised. (1951a, 25)

One of the most interesting points in Childe's argument was that the craftsmen could not easily be accommodated within the kinship social structure of Stone Age society.

Under Stone Stage barbarism security of the person and property is guaranteed by the blood feud – by collective vengeance of the victim's kindred upon the aggressor and his kin. But the itinerant metal-worker has no kinsmen on the spot to avenge him. The new class of specialists do not easily fit into the old social structure organised on a kinship basis. A Bronze Stage can begin only if the mode of production and the organization of society be adjusted to meet these requirements. (1946c, 25)

While in Europe Childe envisaged the exclusion of the craftsman from kinship society, in the Orient he postulated the breakdown of the clan structure and its replacement by class society, that is by groups no longer related by kin but by territory. Here he argued that the concentration of social surplus necessary for the inception of a bronze industry was secured by a divine king and a small class of nobles who appropriated as taxes and rent the tiny surpluses produced by the peasants. Childe considered the social structure in the Oriental Bronze Age to be 'organic' rather than 'mechanical'.

Group members after the specialisation of labour could not all be identified by a common purpose, but held differentiated functions. This 'organic solidarity', however, was achieved by economic classes with different interests; on the one hand a tiny ruling class who annexed the bulk of the social surplus, and on the other the vast majority who were left with a bare subsistence and effectively excluded from the spiritual benefits of civilisation (1950e, 16).

As noted previously Childe's inferences as to the different types of social structure in the Bronze Age were of crucial importance when he came to explain culture change in both the Orient and Europe. However, while he had attempted in 1936 to illustrate how the structure of Bronze Age society had prohibited culture progress in the ancient East it was not until the mid fifties that he used the social structure in Bronze Age Europe as an explanation for the rapid technological progress in the area.

The Iron Age

Childe attempted only a very general analysis of Iron Age economy and social structure. Indeed the Iron Age as a technological and economic stage rarely features in his work as a whole. While he wrote several books and articles specifically on the Stone Age or Bronze Age, for example *The Bronze Age* (1930) and 'The Stone Age Comes to Life' (1954) there is no corresponding work on the Iron Age. Even in his general works the Iron Age plays only a minor role. In *Man Makes Himself* (1936) or 'Early Forms of Society' (1954) the narrative is concluded by the Bronze Age. In *Social Evolution* (1951) although he shows the transition to the Iron Age made by particular cultures in separate regions, he does not refer to the Iron Age as a whole in his quite substantial discussion of the three ages at the beginning of the book. Likewise in *Piecing Together the Past* (1956) the Iron Age is conspicuously absent from his discussion on the three-age system. One is further disappointed to find that in articles such as 'Archaeological Ages as Technological Stages' (1944) and 'The Social Implications of the Three Ages' (1946), that the Iron Age does not receive the same depth of analysis as the Stone or Bronze Age. Indeed in both these articles the primary focus is on the Bronze Age. Nevertheless Childe did in fact argue that during the Iron Age a new type of civilisation different in character from civilisation in the Bronze Age was first firmly established.

Provided they would take the trouble – generally a lot of trouble – almost any community could provide itself with metal from local materials and forge therefrom tools that, however inferior to the best bronze ware, were still a good deal more efficient than stone ones.

Iron was therefore effectively obtainable without the large capital accumulation indispensable for the regular use of copper or bronze. It was in fact obtained by people independent of kings or chieftains concentrating the social surplus, and used in production more freely and widely than bronze had ever been. . . .

A technology based upon metal so easily available could work under relations of production different from those indispensable when copper or bronze was the basis, such extreme concentration was no longer necessary. Now, while monarchies of the Bronze Age type persisted in Egypt, Mesopotamia and, for that matter China, it is a truism of ancient history that many Iron Age societies in Italy, Greece, Syria and Palestine (before Solomon) were organized as republics. (1946c, 30–1)

Childe's reinterpretation of the three ages, then, fundamentally altered his view of the model in the discipline. No longer did he see it as a chronological framework for the classification of cultures but rather as a socio-economic model of the past based on techno-economic criteria. In this context it was to be expected that it should correspond with other socio-economic models of the past especially if these have a similar classificatory basis. Childe himself certainly believed this. In 1951 he writes,

I have spent twenty years trying to give some such values (i.e. economic and sociological) to the traditional 'Ages' and to make these archaeological stages coincide with what sociologists and comparative ethnographers recognised as main stages in cultural evolution. (1951a, 22)

Indeed throughout his career Childe had frequently approached the past using a combination of Lewis Morgan's model of savagery, barbarism and civilisation and the three ages. In *What Happened in History* (1942) for example, he equated savagery with the Palaeolithic as a descriptive label for the hunting-gathering stage of man's evolution, barbarism with the Neolithic for the subsequent food-producing stage and the first two thousand years of civilisation with the Bronze Age. Before attempting to assess how successful Childe was in correlating the two models, it is first of all necessary to examine the main features of the Morgan model. This was basically a sociological model concerned with the development of social institutions from the family to the state. Morgan envisaged an evolution from sexual communism to monogamy, from *gens* to state, from matrilineality to patrilineality. Like Childe's interpretation of the three ages it was based on techno-economic criteria:

Lower savagery	fruit and nut subsistence
Middle savagery	fish subsistence and fire
Upper savagery	bow and arrow
Lower barbarism	pottery
Middle barbarism	domestication of animals (Old World), cultivation of maize, irrigation, adobe and stone architecture (New World)
Upper barbarism	iron tools
Civilization	phonetic alphabet and writing

(Morgan in Harris 1968, 181)

Childe had a great admiration for this nineteenth-century model and while he recognised many of its faults he regarded it as the best attempt of its kind. For Childe Morgan's importance lay in three factors.

> The subject of his investigation is not the evolution of individual institutions isolated from their social context, but the evolution of society as a whole. Secondly, he attempts at the start to determine the order in which the societies that are to document his theses are to be arranged. At least, he laid down in advance the framework of a sequence – the so-called 'ethnical periods' – and formulated criteria by which the position of any observable society in the sequence could be recognised. . . . Finally, the criteria Morgan selected are technological, and therefore comparable to the objects of archaeological study. (1951a, 6–7)

Furthermore Childe believed that the intrinsic importance of Morgan in the history of anthropological theory had been enormously enhanced by the fact that Karl Marx and Friedrich Engels had adopted his scheme (1951a, 9). Neither Marx nor Engels were anthropologists and in seeking source material for their studies on pre-capitalist economic structures it was natural that they should turn to the work of eminent authorities in that field. Morgan's model, based as it was partly on technological criteria, proved to be just the right type of material suitable for conversion into a consistent materialist approach to the past.

> SAVAGERY – the period in which the appropriation of natural products, ready for use, predominated; the things produced by man were, in the main, instruments that facilitated this appropriation.
>
> BARBARISM – the period in which knowledge of cattle breeding and land cultivation was acquired, in which methods of increasing the productivity of nature through human activity were learnt.
>
> CIVILIZATION – the period in which knowledge of the further working-up of natural products, of industry proper, and of art was acquired.
>
> (Engels 1954, 46, orig. 1884)

By 1951, however, Childe had to confess that his socio-economic interpretation of the three ages did not coincide with Morgan's three ethnical periods. While Palaeolithic and Mesolithic society could be placed in Morgan's stage of savagery, and Neolithic societies in the subsequent stage of barbarism, Bronze Age societies could not be so easily equated with civilisation. Here Childe had to admit that there was a wide variety of socio-economic systems founded on this one technological base.

> Bronze Age societies in the Old World are found to differ enormously among themselves in their political and social organization, in their economic structure and even in their level of technological achievement. Many Bronze Age villages in temperate Europe and even in Asia Minor are no larger, nor apparently more articulated, than Neolithic hamlets in the same region. On the other hand, Bronze Age Egyptians, Sumerians, Minoans and Chinese were fully literate and dwelt often in large cities. So this one archaeological Stage covers two major ethnographic or sociological stages – Barbarism and Civilization, as these terms have just been defined. (1951a, 26)

Moreover, he even acknowledged that civilisation was in fact possible without bronze technology, here making one of his rare references to New World civilisations.

It cannot even be contended that the use of metal – for

instance, in imposing industrial specialization and trade or by making advanced transport available – was an essential precondition for Civilization. For in the New World the Mayas, in virtue of their refined calendar and their hiero-glyphic writing, must be deemed to have reached that status. Yet on archaeological criteria they must be labelled Neolithic, since they made no use of metal tools or weapons. . . .

Accordingly the archaeological division between the three Ages provides no serviceable basis for a subdivision of Barbarism into stages. (1951a, 26–7)

The Neolithic and Urban Revolutions

When Childe introduced his functional-economic interpreta-tion of the three ages in 1935, the concept of revolution was clearly an integral part of his scheme. At this time he envisaged three revolutions at the beginning of the Neolithic, Bronze and Iron Ages respectively. These were viewed as transition points of critical importance between the stages.

The first revolutionary advance was made when some group or groups began to cultivate plants and/or to breed food animals. . . . That revolution in human life may be termed the neolithic revolution. . . .

I have tried in my *Bronze Age* to show how the next of the classical 'periods' is delimited by an economic revo-lution of almost equal scope . . . Bronze Age implies an economic revolution which has evoked and provided a living for specialized craftsmen and merchants. . . .

The Iron Age is demarcated by an economic revolution of even more significance. . . . Cheap iron tools opened up new and more fertile lands for settlement and thus made available new supplies of food. Distribution maps vividly illustrate the dramatic expansion of population as a result of the Iron Age Revolution. (1935c, 7–8)

In the following year in *Man Makes Himself* he writes,

The archaeologist's ages correspond roughly to economic stages. Each new 'age' is ushered in by an economic revo-lution of the same kind and having the same efffect as the 'Industrial Revolution' of the eighteenth century. (1936a, 39)

In the same text, however, Childe replaced the Bronze and Iron Age revolutions by the concept of an urban revolution, thus destroying his original neat pattern. Whereas the Neolithic, Bronze and Iron Age revolutions were closely connected to the Neolithic, Bronze and Iron Stages respectively even the term 'urban' was significantly outside the three-age framework. Etymologically it specified the 'urbs' or city as the key feature of the process rather than the change to a particular techno-economic level. Here it should be noted that Childe did in fact quite often associate his urban revolution with Morgan's stage 'civilisation' (1950e). Indeed it can be argued that since 'urbs' is closely related in meaning to civilisation that the urban revolution is more appropriate to the Morgan model than to the three ages. Certainly, as Daniel remarked in 1943, the urban revolution can only be rather uncomfortably accommodated within the three-age structure, by viewing it as the transition to the Bronze Age in Orient and to the Iron Age in Europe (Daniel 1943, 47f.).

The Neolithic Revolution

Childe was aware of the revolutionary implications of food production before he coined the phrase Neolithic revolution. In the first edition of *The Most Ancient East* he writes,

> The greatest moments – that revolution whereby man ceased to be purely parasitic and, with the adoption of agriculture and stock raising, became a creator emancipated from the whims of his environment, and then the discovery of metal and the realization of its properties – have indeed passed before the curtain rises. (1928, 2)

It was not until 1935 in 'Changing Methods and Aims in Prehistory' that he introduced the idea of a Neolithic revolution.

> The first steps in progress that distinguish man from other animals – the control and production of fire and so on – go back to the Old Stone Age. But all palaeolithic peoples relied for sustenance, as far as we know, exclusively on hunting, fishing and collecting. The first revolutionary advance was made when some group or groups began to cultivate plants and/or to breed food animals. Cultivated plants and domesticated animals put the cultivator, the herdsman and the mixed farmer in control of their own food supply; they can within certain limits augment the supply according to demand. And so population can expand to a degree impossible even amongst the most favourably situated hunters like the Magdalenians in the Dordogne or the Kwakiutl in British Columbia. It is one of

92

the many services rendered to prehistory by Elliot Smith to have insisted on the revolutionary contrast between food-gatherers and food-producers. Following his lead Harold Peake and others have proposed equating the beginning of the neolithic with the beginning of food-producing economy. That revolution in human life may be termed the neolithic revolution. Neolithic will mean 'food-producing' and will point a contrast with the food-gathering economy of the Old Stone Age. (1935c, 7))

Here Childe acknowledged the important role which Elliot Smith had played in bringing archaeologists to an understanding of the significance of the changeover from a food-gathering to a food-producing economy. Indeed in 1928 Smith had emphasised that 'it was the agricultural mode of life that furnished the favourable conditions of settled existence, conditions which brought with them the need for such things as represent the material foundation of civilization' (Smith 1928, 37). Prior to food production he believed that man was in a natural state of innocence.

Natural Man is thus revealed as a naked, harmless, truthful child, good-natured, honest and considerate, with an aptitude for pictorial art and craftsmanship. . . . Though timid and friendly, he is always ready to fight for his life. . .

Though skilful and competent, Natural Man displays no innate desire to build houses, or to make clothes, to till the soil or to domesticate animals. He has neither religion nor social organization. (Smith 1928, 26)

Since he held that man was by nature uninventive he sought an explanation for the changeover to food production in environmental stimuli. Here he stressed the unique conditions prevailing in the Nile valley in approximately 4000 B.C.

What was it then, it may be asked, that brought to an end this era of simple life with its complete freedom and peacefulness? From the evidence at our disposal there seems to be very little doubt that the presence of an abundant crop of barley on the banks of the Nile in Upper Egypt was the predisposing factor in creating the vast revolution in the affairs of mankind which prepared the way for the creation of civilization. . . .

It cannot be too strongly emphasised that the whole development was due to the fact that the Ancient Egyptians were favoured with an altogether unprecedented

> type of environment. They enjoyed the privilege of living
> in a rich land which provided them with barley, millet and
> ground nuts, and with ample supplies of meat and game –
> beef, mutton, gazelle; ducks, geese, quails and other
> birds. . . . Is it any wonder that the Egyptians forsook the
> nomadic life and settled in definite places in the valley to
> take advantage of the riches which Nature offered them?
> (Smith 1928, 36–9)

In his later writing Childe was to characterise Elliot Smith's
thesis as disguised theology, labelling his Egyptian cradle of
civilisation as a 'Nilotic Eden' (1951a, 12).

> In the twentieth century the doctrines of Creation and the
> Fall have been revived under the guise of Diffusionism. I
> am sure that Elliot Smith, the founder of the English
> Diffusionist school, had no intention of reviving theo-
> logical dogmas in his polemic against Tylor and his concept
> of evolution. Yet that in effect is what Diffusionism has led
> to. . . . Savages are represented by Diffusionists as totally
> without initiative, without the desire or the capacity for
> inventing a device, a myth or an institution. All the major
> inventions were made but once by some chosen people. . .
> Since no people can civilize itself, civilization must be a
> miracle, the result of supernatural intervention.
> (1951a, 12–13)

Childe argued that Elliot Smith believed he had rationalised
this miracle by reference to the unique environmental circumstances of the Nile, but this he insisted was itself a myth which
was exploded by the discovery of early civilisation in Mesopotamia. Nonetheless despite the vehemence of Childe's attack
against Elliot Smith's thesis there are many points of similarity
between his own explanation of the changeover to food production and that of Smith. Indeed Childe's environmentalist
approach can be seen as merely a broader application of the
same basic thesis. In the first edition of *The Dawn* he explained
both the lack of progress in the Orient to the climatic conditions brought about by the recession of the last glaciation. His
argument, however, was not well developed and the reader is
left to his own devices to assume in what way the environment
of western Asia was 'eminently favourable to cultural progress'
(1925a, 22). In the first edition of *The Most Ancient East*,
however, he is more explicit and after describing the fertile
Oriental parklands during the last glaciation he writes

The pleasant grasslands of North Africa and Southern Asia were naturally as thickly populated by man as the frozen steppes of Europe, and it is reasonable to suspect that in this favourable and indeed stimulating environment man would make greater progress than in the ice-bound north. (1928, 26)

With the retreat of the last glaciation and the subsequent drying up of the grasslands he argued,

That event would certainly tax the ingenuity of the inhabitants of the former grass-land zone to the utmost. Enforced concentration in oases or by the banks of ever more precarious springs and streams would require an intensified search for means of nourishment. Animals and men would be herded together round pools and wadis that were growing increasingly isolated by desert tracts, and such enforced juxtaposition might almost of itself promote that sort of symbiosis between man and beast that is expressed in the word 'domestication'. (1928, 42)

Childe was to retain this argument throughout his entire career. The following passage was written over twenty years later,

Food production – the deliberate cultivation of food plants, especially cereals, and the taming, breeding, and selection of animals – was an economic revolution – the greatest in human history after the mastery of fire. . . . The conditions of incipient desiccation . . . would provide a stimulus towards the adoption of a food-producing economy. Enforced concentration by the banks of streams and shrinking springs would entail an intensive search for means of nourishment. Animals and men would be herded together in oases that were becoming increasingly isolated by desert tracts. Such enforced juxtaposition might promote that sort of symbiosis between man and beast implied in the word 'domestication'. (1952a, 23–5)

As Braidwood later pointed out Childe's environmental determinism was not wholly satisfactory.

There had also been three earlier periods of great glaciers, and long periods of warm weather in between. . . . Thus the forced neighborliness of men, plants and animals in river valleys and oases must also have happened earlier. Why didn't domestication happen earlier too, then? (Braidwood 1951, 86)

Furthermore, the results of Braidwood's field work in the Near

East led him to question the extent of the environmental change at the beginning of the food-producing era.

> In southwestern Asia . . . our colleagues in the natural sciences see no evidence for a radical change in climate or fauna between the levels of the Zarzian and those of the Jarmo or Hassunah phases.
>
> (Braidwood and Howe 1960, 181)

Since Braidwood could find no sufficient cause in the external environment for the changeover to food production, he sought an explanation in man's cultural development, in particular his knowledge of plants and animals.

> In my opinion there is no need to complicate the story with extraneous 'causes'. The food producing revolution seems to have occurred as the culmination of the ever increasing differentiation and specialization of human communities. Around 8000 B.C. the inhabitants of the hills around the fertile crescent had come to know their habitat so well that they were beginning to domesticate the plants and animals they had been collecting and hunting.
>
> (Braidwood 1960, 134)

More recently Binford has suggested that Childe's propinquity theory is in fact one of population disequilibrium (1968, 328f.). Climatic change involves a reduction in the available amount of food in a given area and consequently the balance between food supply and population is disturbed. Like Childe, Binford believes that disequilibrium between population and food supply in a given region may provide a sufficient incentive towards food production, but unlike Childe he does not attribute the disequilibrium to a reduction in food supply brought about by climatic change. Instead he proposes that it was increase in population which caused the disequilibrium.

In Childe's analysis, however, population increase is seen not as a stimulus to, but rather a consequence of, the Neolithic revolution.

> Barbarism or food production, whether by agriculture or stock breeding or the combination of both as mixed farming, initiated the Neolithic Stage. Its beginning is often called the Neolithic revolution. using the term by analogy with the industrial revolution, for there are reasons for supposing that it was followed by a somewhat comparable relative increase in population. Archaeologically, Neolithic villages and settlements are larger than Palaeolithic

and Mesolithic. In ethnography, barbarous populations are generally substantially denser than savage groups.

> In theory, the same area used as pastures, and still more as corn fields or yam gardens, will provide food for more men than the same area used only for hunting and collecting. In theory again, food can be produced for an expanding population merely by extending the cultivated area and by allowing herds and flocks to multiply. (1954b, 43)

Childe assumed a direct relationship between population density and food supply which in turn was determined by 'natural resources, the techniques of their exploitation and the means of transport and food preservation available' (1950e, 4). While he was aware of the difficulties involved in obtaining estimates of prehistoric populations he nevertheless could point to a general population increase during the neolithic stage.

> Even the imperfect data now at our disposal permit of provisional comparisons of population-densities at successive ages or stages. No doubt the chance of a skeleton, a grave or a hut-site surviving is inversely proportional to its antiquity. But even so, the number of palaeolithic and mesolithic skeletons known from France is tiny in comparison to the thousands assigned to the neolithic age. Yet the former have to be distributed over a period of ten or twenty times as long. The comparison gives a distinct if inconclusive indication that the neolithic revolution, the adoption of a food producing economy, did promote an expansion of population as it should on our theory. (1935c, 12)

Recent regional studies such as that of Hole and Flannery (1967) in south-western Iran would tend to support Childe's thesis. Here 0.1 persons per square kilometre were estimated for the late palaeolithic, 1–2 persons per square kilometre for early dry farming and up to 6 or more per square kilometre after irrigation.

It may be, however, that Childe has underestimated the complexity of the retraints on the mechanisms of population growth. In particular cultural restraints such as infanticide, abortion and lactation taboos are now known to contribute to maintaining stable populations (Deevy 1960; Dumond 1965; Birdsell 1958; Halbawchs 1960). At the same time the role of population growth as a contributory factor towards techno-economic change may be more significant than Childe believed (Smith 1972).

In addition to increasing the population Childe saw the Neolithic revolution as providing the circumstances for an economic surplus.

> The Neolithic Revolution had other consequences besides increasing the population. . . . The new economy allowed, and indeed required, the farmer to produce every year more than was needed to keep himself and his family alive. In other words it made possible the regular production of a social surplus. (1950e, 6)

However, he did admit that in exceptional circumstances certain hunters and gathers could achieve a surplus (1954b, 41–2). These cases are, however, perhaps less exceptional than Childe supposed. In the Near East, the home of the Neolithic revolution, two pieces of research may be referred to in this context. First, Harlan's now well-known experiment in Turkey. Here Harlan (1967) harvested a kilo of wild einkorn in an hour and estimated that a family of four could harvest a metric ton in three weeks, more grain than a family could possibly consume in a year. Secondly, Zohary (1969) estimated that in eastern Galilee mixed stands of wild emmer wheat and wild barley would produce 500–800 kilos of grain harvest in rainy years, i.e. that in certain conditions wild wheat and barley form stands as dense as those in a cultivated field.

Recent ethnographic research on subsistence economies of modern hunter-gatherers has also shown that the potential of economic surplus is not restricted to food producing economies. Far from being on the brink of starvation they have an abundance of food resources, notable cases in this context being the Boratse, the Kung bushmen, the Hadza and the Dorobo (Binford 1968, 326).

The Urban Revolution

In Childe's analysis the Neolithic revolution quite clearly indicated an economic change from food gathering to food production and equally clearly marked a transition period between what he saw as two economic stages, the Palaeolithic and the Neolithic. This is not the case with the urban revolution. As noted above the term refers to the urbs or the city as the centre of the process rather than to any specific economic change. Furthermore, the economic stage which the urban revolution initiates is not clearly stated. It may be associated with the beginning of the Bronze Age, or with the beginnings of both the Bronze and Iron Ages, or with the sociological stage civilisation.

Urbanism is not an easy concept to define, and can be approached by a number of avenues, ecological, sociological, functional, etc. (Wheatley 1972). Childe himself employed a 'trait complex' approach by which he hoped to identify the 'urbs' or city by a set of inter-related traits. In 'The Urban Revolution' (1950), his definitive work on urbanism, he listed ten traits common to the oldest cities.

1. *Size:* The first cities were more extensive and more densely populated than previous settlements.

2. *Composition and Function:* In these two aspects the urban population differed from that of any village by the inclusion of full-time specialists, craftsmen, transport workers, merchants, officials and priests.

3. *Surplus:* Each primary producer paid his surplus to the god or king who thus concentrated the surplus. Without this concentration, owing to the low productivity of the rural economy, no effective capital would have been made available.

4. *Monumental Buildings:* These distinguish the city from the village and symbolise the concentration of social surplus.

5. *Unequal Distribution of Social Surplus:* Priests, civil and military leaders and officials absorbed a major share of the concentrated surplus and thus formed 'a ruling class'.

6. *Writing:* Writing was invented in order to facilitate the administration necessitated by the social organisation.

7. *The Invention of Sciences:* The invention of writing in turn allowed the elaboration of the exact and predicative sciences, i.e. of arithmetic, geometry and astrology.

8. *Naturalistic Art:* Other specialists give a new direction to artistic expression. Artists in the early centres of civilisation began to carve, model and draw likenesses of persons or things, not with the naive naturalism of the hunter but according to conceptualised and sophisticated styles.

9. *Trade:* Regular 'foreign' trade in both luxuries and essentials was common to all early civilisations.

10. *State Organisation based on Residence rather than on Kinship:* In the city specialist craftsmen were both provided with raw materials needed for the employment of their skill and also guaranteed security in a state organisation based on residence rather than kinship.

Adams in *The Evolution of Urban Society* (1966) makes two important objections to this type of approach. First he criticises the mixed nature of Childe's set of criteria, and secondly he argues that since the list is descriptive rather than explanatory it is more suitable for the recognition of stages rather than the understanding of process.

> One objection to such listing is that it gives us a mixed bag of characteristics. Some, like monumental architecture, can be unequivocably documented from archaeological evidence but also are known to have been associated occasionally with non-civilized peoples. Others, like exact and predicative sciences, are largely matters of interpretation from evidence that is at best fragmentary and ambiguous. And still others, if not most of Childe's criteria, obviously must have emerged through a gradual, cumulative process not easily permitting distinctions in kind to be kept apart from those merely in degree. Moreover, these characteristics differ radically from one another in their importance as causes, or even as indices, of the Urban Revolution as a whole. The significance of the reappearance of representational art – indeed, its initial appearance insofar as it deals with the human figure – for example is not immediately apparent.
>
> A more basic objection to any such listing is that its eclecticism embraces fundamental contradictions as to purpose. Childe echoes Morgan in seeking to identify the Urban Revolution by a series of traits whose vestiges the specialist can conveniently recognise. This was a reasonable procedure for Morgan's purpose, the initial delineation of a succession of stages, but with Childe, on the other hand, we enter an era in which the emphasis shifted towards providing accounts with explanatory power as well. (Adams 1966, 10–11)

More recently Wheatley (1972, 612) made the important point that there was little functional inter-relationship between the ten traits. Like Adams he viewed these traits as essentially delineatory in nature rather than explanatory and consequently of little value to an understanding of process. It is important to note, however, that both Adams and Wheatley pointed out that in this eclectic list of traits Childe saw the primary causative factors of urbanism as the growth of technology and the increasing availability of food surpluses as deployable capital

(Adams 1968, 12; Wheatley 1972, 612).

Perhaps the most intriguing question arising from Childe's view of urbanism concerns the relationship between bronze metallurgy and the urban revolution, i.e. the extent to which Childe saw this major technological change as playing a causative role in the transition to an urban society. In 1930 Childe published *The Bronze Age* in which he attempted to interpret this archaeological age as a major stage in economic as well as technological development. Not only did bronze metallurgy indicate an important technological breakthrough but it also implied regular and extensive trade (1930a, 7). Furthermore he argued that the development of internal and foreign commerce pre-supposed a degree of political stability (1930a, 9).

In *Man Makes Himself* (1936) Childe listed bronze metallurgy as one of the several inventions which paved the way to urban life.

A second revolution transformed some tiny villages of self-sufficing farmers into populous cities, nourished by secondary industries and foreign trade, and regularly organised as States. Some of the episodes which ushered in this transformation can be discerned, if dimly, by pre-history. The scene of the drama lies in the belt of semi-arid countries between the Nile and the Ganges. Here epoch-making inventions seem to have followed one another with breathless speed, when we recall the slow pace of progress in the millennia before the first revolution or even in the four millennia between the second and the Industrial Revolution of modern times.

Between 6000 and 3000 B.C. man has learnt to harness the force of oxen and of winds, he invents the plough, the wheeled cart and the sailing boat, he discovers the chemical processes involved in smelting copper ores and the physical properties of metals, and he begins to work out an accurate solar calendar. He has thereby equipped himself for urban life, and prepares the way for a civilization which shall require writing, processes of reckoning, and standards of measurement – instruments of a new way of transmitting knowledge and of exact sciences. In no period of history till the days of Galileo was progress in knowledge so rapid or far-reaching discoveries so frequent. (1936a, 118, 119)

In 1942 we find essentially the same argument.

Metallurgy, the wheel, the ox-cart, the pack-ass and the sailing ship provided the foundations for a new economic organization. (1942a, 79)

According to Childe, then, the invention of bronze metallurgy did not in itself bring about urbanism. Rather it was seen as one of several significant technological changes which were to result in the urban revolution. Nevertheless, it is clear that Childe considered it to be the crucial invention. Not only was bronze the first luxury to become a necessity, but it demanded full-time specialisation and the concentration of social surplus on a large scale (1954b, 46). The latter in Childe's eyes was an essential element in the transformation from village to urban life.

Childe argued that the surplus could be accumulated in two ways, neither of which was mutually exclusive.

Either each farming unit must produce more food without a proportionate increase in home consumption, or the number of units must be multiplied so that the little surpluses each of them produces can somehow be pooled to swell a total available for distribution. (1954b, 46)

According to Childe it was the second procedure which led to the urban revolution. In this context he considered that irrigation had played an important role in increasing the yield.

It is obviously no accident that the revolution was first achieved in sub-tropical countries. In them, under intensive cultivation, even a small area will support a large population. In particular, irrigation-farming in the valleys of the Nile, the lower Tigris-Euphrates, and the Indus with its tributaries, yields an exceptionally high return per acre, permitting a considerable density of population. (1954b, 46)

He argued, however, that it was not the increased yield *per se*, but rather the concentration of individual yields which was the critical factor in the urban revolution. Furthermore, he believed that irrigation works required the co-operation of a substantial labour force for digging canals and embankments.

Since Childe's death the role of irrigation in urbanism has been reconsidered. It now generally agreed that the construction and maintenance of simple irrigation systems do not require either large labour forces or elaborate administration. Some scholars nevertheless still consider irrigation farming to be a vital element in the process of urbanism. Flannery, for example, has calculated the percentage of land in Iran suitable for hunting-gathering (30 per cent), dry farming (10 per cent) and irrigation farming (1 per cent). Corresponding to each of these land types he saw important increases in population. He thus argued that it was the widening gap between population size and critical land surface rather than argicultural surplus alone which led to social stratification (Flannery 1972). Another school of thought sees the introduction of large-scale irrigation to be a consequence rather than a cause of the appearance of dynastic state organisation (Adams 1968, 68f.). More recently, however, Joan Oates has pointed out that the situation in reality was probably more of a spiral than an either/or relationship.

> The differentiation of society that was to culminate in the bureaucratic administrations of later Mesopotamia depended intially on food surpluses which irrigation served not only to increase, but for the first time to make secure. This economic situation must have encouraged the social and political developments that in turn made possible more ambitious hydraulic schemes. (Oates 1972, 306)

As with the Neolithic revolution Childe judged the success of his urban revolution with reference to a numerical criterion (1936a, 160f.). However, while he considered it to have been ultimately successful in that it allowed considerable population increase, he was not wholly enthusiastic about the means whereby this success had been attained. As noted previously he argued that the cost was high, i.e. the division of society into economic classes with opposing interests and the suppression of the majority of the people by a small class of kings and priests. Furthermore, he argued that it was the rigidification of the class structure that prohibited further technological progress in the Orient.

4

Historical Theory

Childe was unique among his contemporaries, not because he made historical inferences from the archaeological record, but because of his direct interest in the nature of these inferences, i.e. in historical interpretation and historical explanation. It was during the thirties that he first made it clear that he intended to interpret archaeological data according to a Marxist view of history.

> It is an old-fashioned sort of history that is made up entirely of kings and battles to the exclusion of scientific discoveries and social conditions. And so it would be an old-fashioned prehistory that regarded it as its sole function to trace migrations and to locate the cradles of peoples. History has recently become much less political – less a record of intrigues, battles and revolutions – and more cultural. That is the true meaning of what is mis-called the materialist conception of history – realist conception would as Cole says be better – it puts in the foregound changes in economic organization and scientific discoveries. (1935c, 9–10)

Interestingly, following Cole, he saw Marxism as a realist rather than a materialist outlook. The former in 1934 had argued that the phrase 'materialist conception of history' was fundamentally misleading in that it implied asserting the supremacy of matter over mind, or even of denying the existence of mind altogether (Cole 1934, 14–15). Historical materialism, however, not only accepts the existence of mind or consciousness but sees it as a vital force in the historical process. Cole thus argued as follows,

> Marx called his conception of history 'materialist', because he was determined to mark it off sharply from the metaphysical Idealism of Hegel and his followers. Where he wrote 'materialist' it would be natural in our day to write 'realist', for it is Realism and not Materialism that

we are accustomed to contrast with Idealism as a philosophical point of view. (Cole 1934, 16)

In 1934, Childe visited the u.s.s.r. for the first time, and as he
was later to recall in 'Retrospect' it was then that he began to
appreciate the explanatory potential of Marxism as a model of
the past (1958a, 71–2). Childe, however, was not totally won
over to Soviet theory, in particular he opposed the narrow
evolutionism propagated in the Soviet Union, emphasising the
importance of diffusion as a mechanism of culture change.

Here it is important to keep in mind that during the first half
of the twentieth century, evolutionism and diffusionism were
generally regarded as two entirely separate and distinct
approaches to the historical process based on different philosophical views, not only on the nature of man, but on the
direction of the historical process. Diffusionism was closely
linked to a view of man as uninventive and conservative, culture change taking place only in exceptional circumstances. At
the same time primitive man was generaly seen as spiritually
superior to modern man despite the advance in the latter's
technological equipment. Evolutionism on the other hand embraced a view of man as naturally inclined towards change,
distinguishing 'progress' as the main characteristic feature of
the historical process (Harris 1968; Trigger 1978, 54–74).

The Russian opposition to diffusionism, however, taught
Childe to look more closely at evidence for diffusion.

> Before accepting similar devices, employed by two cul-
> tures, as proofs of diffusion, it is essential first of all to
> determine the chronological relations of the respective
> cultures. . . . The likelihood of diffusion may be increased
> by spatial and quantitative considerations. . . . The dis-
> covery of intermediate spatial links and the multiplication
> of common traits enhance the probability of diffusion
> between two cultures. (1935c, 13–14)

Furthermore, while he accepted diffusion as a mechanism of
change he disassociated himself from contemporary diffusionist schools in England and Germany which he considered to be
methodologically unsound. 'To prove diffusion they too often
relied on superficial resemblances and abstract agreements'
(1935c, 13).

In the following years Childe was to look at the implications
of diffusion in more detail and to attempt to integrate it within
an overall evolutionist viewpoint. Very briefly to anticipate his

main argument Childe held that there was no contradiction between evolution and diffusion. On the contrary, diffusion, which he saw as essentialy 'the pooling of ideas', was effective in 'building up from many sides the cultural capital of mankind' (1937c, 4). In other words it was an important mechanism of social evolution, 'a vital moment in progress itself' (1937c, 14). Throughout his career Childe maintained a firm belief in progress, and it was this belief which linked his thought to that of Marx, Darwin, Spencer and a whole tradition of evolutionary thinking.

In 'Changing Methods and Aims in Prehistory' Childe emphasised that he saw one of the major purposes of history to be the definition of progress. And it was in this context that he felt archaeology to be of paramount importance.

> Evidently archaeology can extend and enrich history equally in the wider domain unilluminated by written documents. And such extension and enrichment is essential if history is worthily to fulfil her functions.

> One of these is surely to define progress. To ask 'have we progressed' is of course meaningless – the question can only be answered in the affirmative. It is for history to say what this progress has consisted in and to provide standards for determining it. But the written record is too short, too broken and too one-sided. To reach a judgement unbiased by private prejudices, one must survey a much wider field than that covered by written documents. In the short time-spans they illumine, accidental ups and downs are relatively so prominent that general tendencies can hardly be isolated from them. Archaeology can survey the vicissitudes of man's material culture, of human economies, not only over the beggarly 5000 years patchily illumined by written records, but over a span of 5000 centuries. It opens up a span wide enough for the accidental features of the landscape to assume their correct proportions. (1935c, 10–11)

In the following year in *Man Makes Himself* (1936) Childe again took up the problem of progress. Basically he was concerned to illustrate that, viewed from an impersonal scientific standpoint, history may still justify a belief in progress in the days of depression as well as in the heyday of Victorian prosperity. In this context he attacked what he termed the pessimistic or mystical attitude conspicuous in the writings of his contemporaries.

> Some are inclined, like the Ancient Greeks and Romans, to look back wistfully to a 'golden age' of primeval simplicity. The German 'historical school' of Roman Catholic missionaries and their archaeological and anthropological instructors have revived and reclothed in scientific terms the medieval doctrine of the 'Fall of Man' through tasting of the tree of knowledge. A similar outlook is implicit in some writings of the English diffusionists. (1936a, 1–2)

At the same time he also criticised the German view of progress which identified advance in human culture with advance in inherent genetic qualities.

> On the other hand, the Fascist philosophy, expounded most openly by Herr Hitler and his academic supporters, but sometimes masquerading as eugenics in Britain and America, identifies progress with a biological evolution no less mystically defined. (1936a, 2)

Childe was thus aware of the subjective nature of the concept of progress.

> As scientists we cannot ask History; 'Have we progressed?' Does the multiplication of mechanical devices represented by aeroplanes, hydroelectric stations, poison gas and submarines, constitute progress? A question so formulated can have no scientific meaning. There is no hope of any agreement upon its answer. That would depend entirely upon the caprice of the enquirer, his economic situation at the time, and even on the state of his health. (1936a, 2–3)

And, in trying to rescue the concept from subjectivism, he argued that the question 'Have we progressed?' should be replaced by the question 'What is progress?', because in his eyes the answer could be given in objective numerical terms.

> It is unscientific to ask 'Have we progressed?', if only because no two people need give the same answer, the personal equation can hardly be eliminated. But it may be legitimate to ask, 'What is progress?' and here the answer may take on something of the numerical form that science so rightly prizes. But now progress becomes what has actually happened – the content of history. The business of the historian would be to bring out the essential and significant in the long and complex series of events with which he is confronted. (1936a, 4)

However, as the above passage clearly shows, what Chlde ended up with was not so much an objective definition of progress but rather a concept of progress stripped of all its connotations of advancement or improvement. It is thus interesting that he was unable to abandon the concept entirely.

The concept of 'progress' as of 'decline' is not a scientific but a metaphysical concept. As Harris has emphasised from a scientific point of view nothing is added or subtracted by calling a particular trend progressive or retrogressive.

> Consider, for example, the change involved in continental glaciations. As the glaciers retreat, the earth may be regarded as exhibiting progress toward a tropical climate, or with no less justification the very same retreat may be regarded as a retrogression away from an arctic climate. By the same token, it is altogether a matter of no scientific consequence for us to describe the recent evolution of American agriculture as progress toward corporate monopolies or retrogression away from small family units. (Harris 1968, 37)

In *Man Makes Himself* Childe emphasised that it was not only the concept of progress which was coloured by the historian's personal viewpoint, but his whole perspective of the past. According to Childe this was particularly true in the context of the political model popular in Britain at that time.

> In fact, ancient history and British history tended to be presented exclusively as political history – a record of the manoeuvres of kings, statesmen, soldiers and religious teachers, of wars and persecutions, of the growth of political institutions and ecclesiastical systems. Incidental allusions were indeed made to economic conditions, scientific discoveries, or artistic movements in each 'period', but the 'periods' were defined in political terms by the names of dynasts or party factions. That sort of history could hardly become scientific. No standard of comparison is manifest in it independent of the prejudices of the individual teacher. The age of Elizabeth is 'golden' primarily to a member of the Church of England. To a Roman Catholic periods when Protestants were burned inevitably seem preferable. (1936a, 6)

It was at this point that he introduced a Marxist view of history as an alternative to the political model, and implicitly as a more objective world viewpoint.

> Fortunately the exclusive claim of political history to the
> title is no longer unchallenged. Marx insisted on the prime
> importance of economic conditions, of the social forces of
> production, and of the applications of science as factors in
> historical change. His realist conception of history is
> gaining acceptance in academic circles remote from the
> party passions inflamed by other aspects of Marxism.
> (1936a, 7)

He does not, however, make it clear in what way the economic
model overcomes the basic subjectivity problem inherent in
patterning the past. Rather this is taken as self-evident and it
was only relatively late in his career that he again raised this
problem. In *Man Makes Himself* Childe's main point about the
Marxist model was its suitability in a prehistoric context.

> This sort of history can naturally be linked up with what is
> termed prehistory. The archaeologist collects, classifies
> and compares the tools and weapons of our ancestors and
> forerunners, examines the houses they built, the fields
> they tilled, the food they ate (or rather discarded). These
> are the tools and instruments of production, characteristic
> of economic systems that no written document describes.
> (1936a, 7)

Here he particularly emphasised the relevance of the Thomsen
model based on the material used for the principal cutting tools
and weapons, arguing that such implements were among the
most important tools of production. Furthermore, according to
Childe, it was this factor which Marxism specified as the determining force in the historical process.

> Realist history insists on their significance in moulding and
> determining social systems and economic organization.
> (1936a, 19)

At this point it would thus seem that Childe was upholding an
essentially technological rather than a sociological or economic
interpretation of Marxism. To a certain extent of course this
was conditioned by the type of material with which he was
working. As a prehistoric archaeologist he had direct technological evidence for the productive forces, the relations of
production or the mode of production being more elusive and
having to be inferred from the archaeological data. Contemporary archaeologists in the Soviet Union, however, were un-
constrained by such considerations and their periodisation of
prehistory was firmly based on the 'relations of production'

(see below, p. 153).

In *What Happened in History*, published in 1942, Childe again discussed the materialist conception of history which this time he characterised as an economic and not a technological model. Here he was concerned to emphasise the reciprocal interplay between ideology and economy, in particular the effect of the former on the latter. Basically he argued that the function of ideology is to hold society together and to lubricate its workings and in this guise it reacts on technology and material equipment (1942a, 23–4). He thus like contemporary functionalists emphasised the integrative, rather than the contradictory, elements in society.

> Even the student of material culture has to study a society as a co-operative organization for producing means to satisfy its needs, for reproducing itself – and for producing new needs. He wants to see its economy working. But the economy affects and is affected by its ideology.
> (1942a, 23f.)

Although, as can be seen from the above discussion, Childe consciously employed a specific historical model from the thirties onwards, his treatment of historical theory before and during the war was limited. Apart from the brief reference to what he termed the realist conception of history in 'Changing Methods and Aims in Prehistory', the subject was confined to summary passages in the introductions to popular texts. It was only after the war that he became deeply involved with historical theory, the first publication on this theme being 'Rational Order in History' (1945) which as the title suggests was concerned with patterns in the historical process.

In this paper, Childe was particularly concerned to illustrate the inadequacies of historical models based upon world outlooks which in his eyes did not admit the reality of change in the historical process. Childe considered the search for a permanent reality outside the historical process to be a feature of most historical models until comparatively recently.

> In the history of historiography, as in that of science, one can trace persistent efforts to find behind the constant flux all too obtrusively experienced in actual life, a permanent reality exempt from change, a durable order behind apparent chaos, a transcendent unity above the struggling mob of events. (1945c, 22)

For Childe it was insignificant whether this unity was seen in secular or theistic terms.

> Now, if you once admit such an order above the process of history, does it make much difference in practice whether you call it Jehovah, or Economic Laws or Evolution? (1945c, 24)

All such theories, according to Childe, eliminated real novelty from the historical process. In ancient Greece for example, he argued that,

> The true reality was . . . conceived as a system of eternal laws from which all real change was eliminated. Human history, too, should become repetitive, cyclical and its constituent events should be reducible to recurrent instances of eternal transcendental laws. (1945c, 23)

Similarly in modern times,

> Buckle and many successors have tried to explain history by geography and meteorology, while the racialists invoke physical anthropology – 'Blood and soil'. Both parties seem to hope that geography and human biology can be reduced to systems of unchanging laws, if not to such exactitude as physics or chemistry. The classical economists, again, had formulated laws that may – or may not – adequately describe the operations of early industrialism. Economic historians have then gone on to elevate these laws into statutes, invested with overriding and compulsive force, and have invoked them to explain the policies of Solomon or Solon! (1945c, 23)

In this context Childe praised the German Idealist philosopher Hegel for his acceptance of novelty and for his view of history as a creative process.

> Hegel really tried to present the history of man and of the universe as a creative process in which genuinely new values, unprecedented qualities and novel events emerged. (1945c, 24)

He was unsuccessful, however, according to Childe, in that he postulated the existence of a transcendent unity above the process.

> For him the process became the self-manifestation of the Absolute Idea acting in accordance with its own eternal nature, the logical 'laws of thought'. The Absolute was thus raised above the process like a sort of deity, so that the process must culminate in a predetermined synthesis. (1945c, 24)

In Childe's eyes the idea of transcendence was unnecessary, since for him history was essentially a self-sufficient process with its own inherent order.

> The historical process is untrammelled by any external laws, but creates its own laws. It has not to conform to any rigid mathematical order, but yet manifests a growing order which reason can partially comprehend. (1945c, 25)

Here Childe emphasised man's difficulty in comprehending this order, arguing that it was not expressible by laws of the same type as physical or chemical laws which can be regarded as immutable for specific practical purposes. According to Childe the laws of history (here he included Darwin's principle of natural selection) had little predictive value.

> From Darwin's principle of selection or from Marx's materialist conception you cannot deduce a particular event, as you can from the law of gravity. They merely provide clues for disentangling order in seeming chaos. With the aid of such conceptions the historian can define *tendencies*, not uniformities. (1945c, 26)

Nevertheless, like Marx, Childe did believe that man could become conscious of his role in the historical process and thus enter upon a new stage in his development.

> We can at least conceive of an historical order consciously developed by the rational co-operation of its human agents in the process. That, I suppose, is what Marx meant in calling contemporary society 'the closing chapter in the *prehistoric* stage of human society'. (1945c, 26)

In *History*, published two years later in 1947, Childe began by contrasting scientific and sociological laws. While the former could be tested empirically in the laboratory, this was not the case with the latter.

> Now it is all too true that no one can conduct such experiments in economics, politics or international organization. We cannot in practice frame conditions so as to isolate one factor and thus discover a single 'cause' as that word is understood in experimental physics, genetics or medicine. So-called experiments like the League of Nations, the Builders' Guild and the various Co-operative Commonwealths fall far short of the conditions obtainable in a laboratory. . . . Even a comparative sociology aiming at the establishment of general rules and general scheme recurrent in many 'instances', the differences between

which can be ignored, . . . can make little headway. On the one hand the number of observed and observable instances is very limited; on the other it is questionable how far these instances are genuinely independent. (1947b, 2f.)

It should be emphasised that for Childe the value of a scientific law was that it provided a maxim for action (1947b, 3). Consequently as man's scientific knowledge had developed so had the practical application of that knowledge in the world.

Notoriously man's control over external nature had been achieved through knowledge of nature. It has progressed hand in hand with the systemization of such knowledge in the natural sciences. And advance has been fastest where the results of the experimental sciences – geometry, mechanics, physics and chemistry – can be applied and has been accelerated by the adoption of experimental methods in other sciences – medicine, genetics, agronomy. (1947b, 2)

And here he suggested that man's lack of success in the social sphere was due to his inability to comprehend the workings of society.

A reasonable inference has been that the painful discrepancy between humanity's control over the external environment and its incapacity to control the social environment is due to the absence of any science of society, the failure of sociology to become genuinely empirical and the impossibility of conducting experiments under laboratory conditions in human relationships. (1947b, 2)

Childe, however, was not wholly pessimistic about the possibility of achieving laws of history for, while it lacked laboratory conditions for practical experimentation,

Mankind ever since its first emergence has been continually experimenting not only in controlling external nature, but also in organizing that control co-operatively. The results of these experiments are embodied on the one hand in the archaeological record – the concrete relics and monuments of the past – and on the other hand in documents transmitted orally, pictorially or best of all in writing. (1947b, 3)

History, then was the scientific study of all these sources. In Childe's words,

History . . . should yield a science of progress though not necessarily an exact science, like physics, nor an abstract

descriptive science, like anatomy. It should, in other
words, disclose, if not mathematical laws or a static
general scheme, an order in its own way as intelligible as
that of astronomy or anatomy. (1947b, 3)

It is important to consider the implications of Childe's view
of the historical process in the context of the possibility of the
construction of historical laws. On the one hand he firmly
rejects the possibility of achieving historical laws with any
predicative value since if this were the case it would of course
contradict his basic premise concerning the truly creative
quality of the historical process. However, on the other, he
does not wish to say that the attempt to discover historical laws
is of no value. Indeed he emphasises that there is a pattern in
the historical process which can be comprehended by reason.
For Childe, if there was no logical pattern in history, the study
of history would be superfluous.

The historian's business would be to ascertain the happenings that are interesting and to describe them in chronological sequence and in an artistic literary form.

If this be so, it is hard to see why one should study
history. If the aim be to interest the reader why not invent
your incidents like a novelist. (1947b, 33)

According to Childe then, the aim of the historian was to
discover patterns in the historical process, not merely to record
or describe events, and to emphasise this point he distinguished
between chronicle and history.

The former records 'what was done and in what year it
happened'; history must exhibit also 'the reasons and
causes of events'. History, in fact, must possess an order
beyond mere succession in time. (1947b, 34)

In *History* the bulk of the text comprises an analysis of four
different views of historical order commencing with the theological conception and concluding with historical materialism.
Firstly, however, Childe was concerned to illustrate the role of
the historian in a tradition of historiography. Basically he made
two main points here; first that the historian has almost always
belonged to the ruling class or at least been closely identified
with it.

The first Sumerian clerks were drawn from the temple
priesthood and servants of the city god, who was also
the largest landowner in each city-state. . . . In Egypt,
where the pharaoh was an actual god, the clerks were his

officials or agents of his nobles. . . .

The clerks of the Middle Ages were in much the same position as Sumerian scribes; . . . In Greece and the Roman empire . . . the authors of histories were generally citizens and well-to-do citizens at that. . . . Even in contemporary Britain . . . the principal market for history-books is formed by the ruling class and its favoured dependants and imitators in the middle classes. (1947b, 21–2)

By beginning with an analysis of the class position of the historian Childe was adopting a classic Marxist approach to historical theory. Marx himself particularly emphasised the class nature of knowledge.

The ideas of the ruling class are in every age, the ruling ideas: i.e. the class which is the dominant *material* force in society is at the same time its dominant *intellectual* force. (Marx (1845) in Bottomore and Rubel 1956, 78)

And this was echoed to a greater or less extent by a whole tradition of his successors (Jordan 1967).

Secondly, Childe argued that to write history must necessarily involve selection by the historian as to what is to be regarded as important or memorable. Here he emphasised that this selection was conditioned by the social environment of the historian, in particular, his social class.

Now no chronicler nor historian can attempt to record all events; from the superfluity of happenings he must select what he regards as memorable. His selection is determined to a very small extent by his personal idiosyncracies, but on the whole by tradition and social interests. Indeed, save for personal memoirs and diaries, the standard of the memorable is a social one, dictated by interests shared by the whole community, or more precisely by the ruling class in each community. (1947b, 22)

At this point Childe was unconcerned with the problem of subjectivity, arguing that,

It is just no good demanding that history should be unbiased. The writer cannot help being influenced by the interests and prejudices of the society to which he belongs – his class, his nation, his Church. (1947b, 22)

It should be noted, however, that later, when he did go further into the problem, he seemed to exempt Marxism from the subjectivity dilemma (1949c, 309)

As indicated above Childe's main concern in *History* was to analyse four major conceptions of historical order which he categorised as follows,

1. 'The theological and magical conceptions of historical order';
2. 'Naturalistic theories of historical order';
3. 'History as a comparative science'
4. 'History as a creative process'.

Before going on to consider the content of these categories however, it is interesting to examine the classification itself, one of the most striking features of the system being the close relationship between the different categories and broad philosophical world outlooks.

The theological and magical (the first grouping) is closely associated with idealism in the broadest sense as the world outlook in which 'spirit' or 'mind' is viewed as the primary reality and matter as secondary. Furthermore, the naturalistic theories of historical order and history as a comparative science (the second and third groupings) can be linked with empiricism where matter is viewed as primary and mind as secondary. Finally, history as a creative process, i.e. Marxism (the fourth grouping) is closely associated with dialectical materialism. Unfortunately, Childe himself does not explicitly define the basis of his classification and thus the relationship between his historical orders and philosophical world-viewpoints has to be inferred from the text.

This, however, is not difficult, and in reviewing *History* for *The Modern Quarterly*, George Thomson was quick to recognise the pattern to Childe's work. Indeed he does not avoid the temptation to rationalise it, presenting it as a categorisation clearly based on three different philosophical systems.

> The greater part of the book is devoted to an examination of three different conceptions of historical order, the 'theological', the 'naturalistic', and the 'scientific', corresponding to subjective idealism, mechanical materialism and Marxism. (Thomson, 267)

In doing so he thus makes explicit what is implicit in the text. At the same time, while he undoubtedly makes a neat equation between Childe's categories and the philosophical systems underlying them, he misrepresents Childe's own approach which was not quite so clear-cut nor consistent. As noted above, Childe distinguished four main types of historical order, the theological, the naturalistic, the comparative and the creative, not three. In order to make his equation Thomson had therefore to subsume the chapter on history as a comparative science under naturalistic theories. Childe, however, preferred to make a distinction. For Childe 'comparative' theories were not 'naturalistic' in that they did not attempt to apply the laws of the natural sciences to the historical process but sought to generate their own descriptive laws based on comparisons between discrete sections of the historical process. The issue is complicated, however, by the fact that Childe includes cyclical theories in both categories. There would thus seem to be some grounds for Thomson's rationalisation.

1. Theological and Magical Conceptions of Historical Order

Childe's main objection to the theological conceptions of history was that the source of order in the historical process was regarded as extrinsic and not intrinsic to that process. Thus it was in Childe's eyes unverifiable by the scientific method and for that reason rejected by him.

> The Divine Government of the world certainly gives unity to history, all significant historical events are reduced to effects of one single cause – God's Will. But the unifying principle cannot be demonstrated by history or deduced from it, but has to be imported from without. It is apprehended by faith, not by reason. It has accordingly no place in any conceivable science of history, but belongs where it began in the pre-scientific era. (1947b, 36–7)

Childe differentiated 'magic' from 'religion' as follows,

> Magic is a way of making people believe they are going to get what they want, whereas religion is a system for persuading them that they ought to want what they get. (1947b, 37)

Consequently he argued that magic is more primitive and older than religion. Childe treated the 'great man' theory of history as magical, which at first sight seems rather odd. The reason, however, goes back to the position of the divine king in ancient history.

> In the theocratic monarchies of Bronze Age Egypt, Mesopotamia and China, the king was not only the author of law and the sustainer of social order, he was also regarded as responsible for the material welfare of the kingdom. By magic rites that he alone could perform, the Egyptian pharoah ensured the rising of the sun, the annual flood of

the Nile and in general the fertility of crops, herds and game. . . .

It would be perfectly reasonable on such a theory to regard the king as the one efficient cause of all historical events. The ancient royal annals are thus the first expressions of the still popular great Man theory of history. (1947b, 37–8)

Childe saw the 'great man' theory of modern times to be a continuation of the earlier viewpoint even although by this time the 'great man' had been freed from the dependence on God's government. And here he makes it clear that he considered the thesis to negate the possibility of patterning the past.

Plainly if such cataclysmic personalities have mysteriously emerged from time to time and have 'changed the course of history' and 'turned it into a new channel' any conception of an historical order must go by the board. (1947b, 40)

In Childe's eyes the fundamental defect of the 'great man' thesis was that it ignored the social environment, the economic context and the technological basis from which the 'great man' arose and in which he operated. He was presented as a 'Jack-in-the-box' who emerges miraculously from the unknown to interrupt the real continuity of history. In this context Childe tended to reduce the importance of the 'great man' and quotes from Engels to support his thesis, 'in default of a Napoleon, another would have filled his place' (1947b, 42). While Childe admitted that this was a hypothetical argument incapable of being tested, he emphasised that 'the objective fact in history is that when a man was necessary he was found' (1947b, 42).

It is relevant here to draw attention to Childe's view of the role of the inventor. Again he emphasised the importance of the society as a whole rather than the individual. For example he saw Watt's contribution towards the steam engine as small in comparison to the 'social capital' to which he contributed, that is, the accumulated inventions and discoveries that society had transmitted to him from the latest improvements in iron-founding and valves to the discovery of the control of fire itself in the Old Stone Age (1947b, 12)

2. Naturalistic Theories of History

Under naturalistic theories of historical order Childe deals with four main types of historical order which he terms geometrical, geographical, anthropological and political. Childe defined as naturalistic all theories that either attempt to depict historical events as instances of immutable laws comparable to the laws of mathematics or astronomy, or which represent the historical order by an abstract but eternal theme or chart (1947b, 43)

Geometrical History. Childe interpreted a geometrical view of history as one in which the past is viewed in terms of mathematical rules. Here he gives the example of the cyclical history first expounded in classical antiquity and made popular in his own day by Spengler. According to this view the historical process is seen to describe a circular not an onward-going path. Again as with the great man thesis Childe's main objection is that it ignores the technological and economic basis of society.

> As soon as the historian extends his survey to embrace science, technology and even those aspects of strategy that are directly dependent upon technology the superficiality of analogies between the several periods of man's history is laid bare.
>
> In these domains it is perfectly obvious that history does not describe a circle but is a cumulative process. And that is really just as true of every aspect of history. (1947b, 46)

Geographical History. Basically Childe argued that geographical environment, while an important factor in explaining the variety of human cultures, could not explain historical change. For example, in Childe's words,

> Look how long it was before the inhabitants of Britain began to seriously utilise coal for fuel though its combustible properties had been known since the Bronze Age some three thousand years ago! (1947b, 49–50)

Geographical environment, then, according to Childe, should be taken into account when attempting to explain historical processes but only as a background for historical development, not as a decisive governing factor. While Childe elsewhere stressed that he saw culture as an adaptation to the environment, here he makes it clear that he viewed the relationship between the two as a reciprocal process. Not only have men been adapting to their environment, but 'throughout their history have been experimenting with increasing success in adapting their environment – even the climate – to their habits and needs' (1947b, 50).

Again this is a classic materialist stance summarising the root of Marx's dialectical method, i.e. the reciprocal interaction between man and nature. Basically Marx argued that the environment was a significant factor in shaping man's nature. However, unlike empiricists who saw man's role as purely passive, he stressed man's practical activity in changing his environment and thus, at the same time, in changing his own nature (Schmidt 1967; Jordan 1967, 16–64).

Anthropological History. What Childe termed the 'anthropological' conception of history was basically the thesis that the inherent qualities of the different races of mankind are fixed in character. According to Childe not only was this an old belief stretching back to the biblical notion of a chosen people, but from the beginning it was closely associated with the belief in the inherent superiority of certain peoples or races. Furthermore, he emphasised that this in turn was used as justification for many racialist policies throughout history (1947b, 50–7).

Childe argued that with the publication of Darwin's theory of evolution last century, the anthropological conception of history had gained a quasi-scientific status owing to the misapplication of biological concepts to the historical process. As noted previously he was deeply concerned about the role of such theories in contemporary politics and thus saw it as a matter of practical as well as academic importance to clearly analyse the relationship between biological and cultural evolution.

History as a department of political economy. Childe traced the laws of political economy from the Renaissance and from the rise of a new class of bourgeoisie. Here he argued that these laws were all based on a few *'a priori'* truths, one of which, the premise of self-interested motivation, gave rise to the concept of economic man.

> By exaggerating this tendency of Humanism and idealizing its product the bourgeois economists of the Industrial Revolution in England created a monster, Economic Man. From his supposed 'nature' they deduced 'eternal laws' that ought to govern the activities of all human societies in producing and exchanging goods as Newton's laws governed the motions of planets and billiard balls. (1947b, 57)

Childe made two criticisms of this type of economic interpretation of history. First he questioned the basic premise of 'economic man' motivated only by materialistic desires, pointing out that it was being challenged even in its own day. Unfortunately, however, Childe does not explicitly state why he considered the concept to be a myth but takes it to be self-evident. This is particularly regrettable in that Childe himself had been strongly influenced by economic determinism, especially during the thirties and early forties when he wrote *Man Makes Himself* and *What Happened in History*.

Secondly, Childe argued that while these laws were scientific in that they were based on observed economic processes, they only applied to one given system, capitalism, and could not be extended to other economic periods.

> In so far as economic laws were genuinely scientific, i.e. were correct descriptions of how goods were actually produced and exchanged, they only applied to a given economic system. . . .
>
> Adam Smith and his immediate successors were, in fact, trying to describe capitalism in the early days of the Industrial Revolution. . . . They were in truth the academic champions of the rising class of capitalist manufacturers against the still dominant landed aristocracy. Some of their successors in Britain and still more in America have championed the same class against the workers in trade unions and in the socialist movement. All assume explicitly a free movement of goods and an equal mobility of labour and therefore tacitly modern means of transport and communications and legal freedom for workers and employers. It would be a manifest absurdity to apply deductions from such technological and sociological assumptions to, say the early Middle Ages when land transport was confined to pack-horses and peasants were tied to the soil. (1947b, 58–9)

Here Childe quotes from a postscript to *Das Capital* in support of his thesis,

> Marx, of course, 'expressly denies that the general laws of economic life are one and the same no matter whether they are applied to the present or the past. According to him every economic period has laws of its own.
> (1947b, 58)

3. History as a Comparative Science

Under this heading Childe grouped two different historical conceptions, the 'cyclical' which he discussed in the previous chapter and the 'parallelistic'. According to Childe both were similar in that they were based on comparisons between different sections of the historical process treated as discrete units.

> If human history could be cut up into a number of consecutive or parallel slices, each might be treated as an instance or an example of generalized history. By comparing them we should discover recurrent features common to all the instances examined. Then, making abstraction of or ignoring differences, we should be left with a general chart or specific description of abstract history. (1947b, 61)

Childe had relatively little to add to his previous rejection of the cyclical method except to note that it had, in his eyes, been refuted in practice. Here he was specifically referring to Spengler's predictions in *The Decline and Fall of the West* where he foresaw the rise of revived Caesarism – 'a Germanic totalitarian world-state foreshadowing even in detail that New Order which Herr Hitler tried in 1939 to impose on a curiously ungrateful world' (1947b, 62). Childe took the defeat of Hitler in 1945 to be the experimental refutation of not only Spengler's thesis but also of the cyclical thesis as a whole.

Childe's main criticism of the parallelistic view of history was that the historical process was a unified interrelated whole, not a series of discrete sections.

> Is it legitimate or profitable to carve history into bits, label them 'civilizations' and then treat them as distinct and independent instances of general laws? Are the bits thus isolated really separate representatives of a species from a comparison of which an inductive description can be constructed like the anatomical chart of the human body based on a dissection of a number of distinct bodies? Are Toynbee's 'civilizations' not rather like the several limbs or organs of one such body? (1947b, 63)

Here he argued that in order to justify the isolation of the units, Toynbee had to minimise the relationships between them. Furthermore, Childe restated the argument that he had originally made against the cyclical interpretation of history.

> In brief, to legitimise the comparative method and make its inferences plausible Toynbee, like Spengler has to ignore just those human activities that in history are unambiguously cumulative and revolutionary. (1947b, 64)

It is worthy of note that in 'The History of Civilization',

published in *Antiquity* 1941, Childe has proposed an alternative to this type of historical structuring. Basically he suggested replacing the politico-geographical units by archaeological periods. This he suggested would allow comparisons between civilisations and would not obscure their interrelations. For example Sumerian, Egyptian and Indus civilisations could be viewed as different aspects of Bronze Age civilisation rather than totally unrelated. Furthermore he argued that with the archaeological framework the progressive enlargement of the continuum leading to modern civilisation could be graphically traced. This was obviously very important to Childe, for as noted previously much of his research was concerned ultimately with the relationship between modern civilisation and its prehistoric precedents.

4. History as a Creative Process

In the final chapter Childe gives a short analysis of Marxist historical theory which he considered to be the only theory of history which accepted both the changeful nature of the historical process and its self-sufficiency. Thus in these two fundamental aspects Marxist historical theory was based on a philosophical world-outlook which coincide with Childe's own. This point perhaps needs emphasising since his rejection of the various historical theories other than Marxism was on account of their failure to present the historical process in these terms.

In *History*, Childe makes it clear that he saw Marxism as basically a technological model.

> Now the simplest aspect of historical order is . . . the progressive extension of humanity's control over external nature by the invention and discovery of more efficient tools and processes. Marx and Engels were the first to remark that this *technological* development is the foundation for the whole of history, conditioning and limiting all other human activities. (1947b, 69–70; my emphasis)

He did not, however, deny the importance of social relations in the productive processes.

> Indeed, the whole productive activity in which tools or machines are used for the provision and distribution of food, warmth and other human needs in all known societies and at every period of recorded history is and has been a social activity involving the co-operation of smaller or greater numbers of people. Whether you like it or not,

you must secure the co-operation of your baker and through him of an indefinite chain of other persons right down to the wheat growers of Manitoba and Iowa if you want a loaf. (1947b, 70)

And here Childe quotes from Marx in support of his thesis,

In the social production of their livelihood men enter into definite relations that are necessary and independent of their wills; these relations of production correspond to a definite stage in the development of their material forces of production. The sum total of these relations of production constitutes the economic structure of society, the real basis on which is reared a legal and political superstructure and to which correspond definite forms of social consciousness. (1947b, 71)

The above passage from the *Preface* to *The Critique of Political Economy* is generally recognised as Marx's classic statement on the materialist principle of history, and usually it is taken to represent an economic, not a technological, interpretation of history. It is thus interesting that Childe interpreted it in technological terms.

Thus Marxism goes on to assert that all constitutions, laws, religions and other so-called spiritual results of man's historical activity are in the long run determined by the material forces of production – tools and machines – together with, of course, natural resources and skills to operate them. Thus the Materialist Conception offers a clue for the analysis of the data of history and opens up the prospect of reducing its phenomena to an easily comprehensible order. (1947b, 71–2)

Lilley in his review of *History* in *The Modern Quarterly* has argued that Childe misinterpreted this particular passage (1949, 264). For here Marx clearly states that it is the economic structure as a whole that constitutes the real foundation of society. Childe's statement, however, would confine the determining element in society to the forces of production, i.e. to the technology, together with the skills required to operate it. It should be pointed out, however, that Childe was not alone in upholding a technological interpretation of Marxism, and indeed there are certain passages in Marx that can be interpreted in this way (Acton 1955). By the majority of its exponents, however, Marxism is usually considered to be an economic rather than a purely technological model (Saville 1973).

In explaining what he considered to be the major principle of Marxism, i.e. its technological determinism, Childe warned that this clue was not to be used slavishly.

A quite superficial survey of history would disclose tragic discrepancies between progressive technology and moribund political or religious institutions. In the first place, 'at a certain stage in their development the productive forces of society come into contradiction with the existing relations of production, i.e. in legal terms, with the property relations, within which they have worked before. From the forms of development of the forces of production, these relations turn into their fetters'.

(1947b, 72, citing Marx 1859)

Here he drew attention to the Marxist theory of revolution as a means of breaking the 'fetters' on the productive forces. Childe, however, emphasised that although this was desirable it was not inevitable, and in this context he gives the example of the stagnation of certain Bronze Age societies.

In Mesopotamia, Egypt and China theocratic despotism, relations of production appropriate to the productive forces of the Bronze Age, persisted into the Iron Age. They effectively fettered the exploitation of the new forces represented by iron with the result that technology also stagnated. The whole life of these societies stagnated too, the first two eventually perished altogether. From a Marxian analysis all that one can deduce is the dilemma – *revolution or paralysis*. History does not disclose an unfaltering march to a predetermined goal. The materialist conception implies that, if science and technology are to progress, the relations of production must be adjusted accordingly. (1947b, 73)

In another review of *History* in *The Modern Quarterly* (1949) Christopher Hill criticised Childe's treatment of revolution, arguing that he did not give sufficient emphasis to the form that the revolution would take. While Childe saw it in terms of 'adjustment' between the productive forces and the productive relations, Hill characterised it as essentially a class struggle. Furthermore he argued that Childe did not clearly analyse the concept of class. This criticism was echoed and extended by Thomson, who held that Childe did not analyse the various historical orders in terms of their class basis, and for him this was the main weakness of the text (Thomson 1949, 267).

While Childe perhaps did not give as much emphasis to the class struggle as some of his Marxist contemporaries would have liked, it is not true that he did not understand either the role of class in society or its relationship to ideology. As noted previously one of his first priorities in *History* was to analyse the class position of the historian in the development of historical studies. In particular he emphasised that the historian's outlook was conditioned by the social class to which he belonged, this usually being the ruling class (see above p.115ff.).

Childe's treatment of the notion of class lacked the bitter polemic which surrounded much of the Marxist literature at that time, and could have been interpreted by his contemporaries as devoid of revolutionary zeal. Today works containing the latter quality are often sadly dated, the revolutionary spirit being seen as dogmatism and adherence to the party line rather than a true understanding of Marxism. One of the enduring merits of Childe's work is that while obviously sympathetic to a Marxist viewpoint it never descends into anti-capitalist propaganda.

In *History*, as in *What Happened in History*, Childe was careful to emphasise the important role of ideology in the historical process. Here, he was particularly concerned with its capacity to hinder technological progress.

> Ideologies, religious creeds, national loyalties and so on may very seriously impede progress. . . . History bristles with examples of the hindrances imposed by superstitions on science and its applications; the Church's ban upon the Copernican theory and Islam's opposition to printing are notorious cases. (1947b, 76)

Childe did, however, admit that ideology could in fact be progressive and thus aid technological development, and here he quotes from Stalin in support of this claim,

> There are new and advanced ideas that serve the advanced forces of society. Their significance lies in the fact that they facilitate the progress of society, and is the greater, the more accurately they reflect the needs of development of the material life of society. New social ideas and theories indeed arise only after the development of its material life has set new tasks before society. But once they have arisen, they become a most potent force which furthers the material progress of society. (1947b, 76)

It should be noted at this point that Childe's reading of Marxism was not confined only to Marx; he was also acquainted with the work of Engels, Lenin and Stalin, and in *History* he quotes from all these sources. While many scholars in the west did not acknowledge the latter as source material for Marxism, Childe seemed at this time to have respect not only for his writings but also for his role as a politician.

As indicated above Childe's view of the creative, changeful nature of reality negated the possibility of historical models with any predictive potential. Thus, unlike many of his Marxist contemporaries Childe denied that historical materialism could foresee the future course of world history,

> No theory of history can foretell what new discoveries will thereby be put at the disposal of society nor precisely what economic organization or political institutions will be suited to their exploitation. Analysed from the standpoint of dialectical materialism history will show how institutions and beliefs have, in fact, in the past been related to technological and scientific developments. (1947b, 83)

At the same time, however, he did not wish to push this point too far, and argued somewhat optimistically that Stalin, using the principles of historical materialism, had successfully predicted the course of world history.

> Scientific history makes no claim to be a sort of astrology to predict the outcome of a particular race or an individual battle for the profit of sportive or militaristic speculators. Its study, on the other hand, will enable the sober citizen to discern the pattern the process has been weaving in the past and therefrom to estimate how it may be continued in the immediate future. One great statesman of today has successfully foreseen the course of world history and him we have just quoted as an exponent of Marxist historiography. (1947b, 83)

Childe's attitude towards prediction is thus ambivalent. At the heart of the problem was his insistence on the wholly creative quality of reality which, if pressed to its logical conclusion, would certainly negate the possibility of historical laws. Obviously if reality was totally creative, constantly bringing forth genuine novelties, no existing laws could encompass these emergent qualities. It was Childe's strict adherence to this philosophical belief which separated him from his Marxist contemporaries who claimed that Marxism did in fact have some predictive value. Indeed the latter maintained that they were able to foresee the resolution of the contradictions in the historical process in a stage of world communism which was regarded as the inevitable outcome of the historical process according to the laws of dialectical materialism.

However, while Childe could not accept this he did not wish to deny that there was a pattern to the historical process or that the construction of laws was not a suitable goal for historians. As noted above, Childe differentiated historical laws from scientific laws which have a high predictive potential. Historical laws on the other hand were just shorthand descriptions of the way in which historical changes came about. They neither cause nor govern these changes but serve to limit the range of incalculable factors without excluding such altogether.

It is important to note that Childe believed that archaeology could contribute to the construction of historical laws. While he did not consider the possibility of it generating its own laws, he held that it was a useful tool for testing theories developed in other disciplines, especially those which lacked archaeology's time perspective (1946d). In particular he considered that it could test the evolutionary schemes of nineteenth-century anthropologists which were constructed on comparisons between contemporary primitive societies. While Childe criticised the comparative method in that it transformed an observable logical geographical scheme into a hypothetical chronological one, he did not believe that this invalidated the hypothesis of social evolution. Like all scientific hypotheses these needed to be tested by observation and it was in this context that archaeology could play a crucial role.

> Now the archaeological record discloses sequences of . . . cultures stratigraphically established, in several areas. In other words, it reveals the chronological order in which societies have appeared. How far does this 'observable scheme' really provide the basis for a 'logical' one? Let us compare homotaxial cultures – that is cultures occupying the same relative positions in the several observed sequences – to ascertain whether the agreements between them can be generalized as stages in cultural evolution, the evolution of Society in the abstract. (1951a, 16)

Here Childe especially wished to test Lewis Morgan's evolutionary scheme which he considered to be the best of its kind to date. As noted above (pp.89ff.) Morgan envisaged human history as three major ethnical periods, savagery, barbarism and civilisation, of which the first two were further subdivided into three sub-periods, lower, middle and upper. Morgan was also interested in the development of the family structure and in this sphere he recognised five successive forms; (1) the consanguine; (2) the punaluan; (3) the syndyasmian; (4) the patriarchal; and (5) the monogamian. Basically this was an evolution from group marriage to the modern nuclear unit. In terms of kinship Morgan recognised the following sequence: (1) Malayan; (2) Turanian-Ganowanian and (3) Aryan-Semitic, which in modern classification correspond to Hawaiian, Iroquois and Eskimo types. As regards social structure the sequence begins with the first two stages of the family, a promiscuous horde, followed by one in which brothers and sisters are forbidden to marry. The next phase is dominated by matrisibs. These combine to form phratries which in turn combine to form tribes and then confederacies. All of these, it should be noted, were distinguished from true political organisation based on reckoning of rights and property relations. The true political units were the township, the county and the state.

As Harris has pointed out Morgan's approach is a remarkable attempt to co-ordinate many different levels of society in one comprehensive scheme.

> The overall effect therefore is of a diachronic and synchronic system of unprecedented structural and chronological scope. The overall movement from systems based on sex and kinship to those based on territoriality and property was connected by a series of negative and positive feedbacks to family form, kinship terminology and the technological criteria of the ethnical periods.
> (Harris 1968, 182)

Today in the light of new evidence Morgan's scheme can be seen to be untenable in many respects. Nevertheless, as Eleanor Leacock has noted, his three major ethnical periods have stood the test of time.

> In spite of the disfavour into which Morgan's work fell, his general sequence of stages has been written into our understanding of prehistory and interpretation of archaeological remains, as a glance at any introductory anthropology text will indicate. (Leacock 1963, lxi)

Childe portrayed Morgan as a parallel evolutionist in the nineteenth-century vein, where cultures are seen to evolve to and from similar conditions in tandem. In *Social Evolution* then, the aim of the text was to use the culture sequences in four different geographical regions, (1) temperate Europe, (2) the Mediterranean zone, (3) the Nile valley and (4) Mesopotamia as empirical examples against which to test the thesis of parallel evolution.

In comparing them to see if they exhibited uniformity or parallelism in their transition from barbarism to civilisation, Childe argued that although the starting point – savagery – and the end result – civilisation – were abstractly similar, in each case the intervening steps did not exhibit even an abstract parallelism. For example, as regards the rural economy,

> In Tasian and Badarian Egypt farming was at best on a par with, and perhaps even subordinate to, the food-gathering activities of hunting, fishing and collecting; in the sequel the relative importance of hunting rapidly declined. In temperate Europe we saw just the reverse: in central and Western Europe hunting was relatively less important in Neolithic stage i than in the succeeding stage ii. . . . Again, in Greece as well as in Hither Asia and Egypt the first definable rural economy was organised so as to permit really sedentary farming. . . . In temperate Europe shifting cultivation was the rule throughout the Neolithic and most of the Bronze stages. . . . In the last-named area we observed a separation of the more pastoral from the agricultural communities; nothing parallel was disclosed by archaeology in Egypt or Mesopotamia. . . .
>
> So the observed developments in rural economy do not run parallel; they cannot therefore be used to define stages common to all the sequences examined. . . . In fine, the development of barbarians' rural economies in the regions surveyed exhibits not parallelism but divergence and convergence. (1951a, 161–2)

From here Childe goes on to argue that the same is true as regards the social structure.

> The fragmentary record of the development of social institutions in the several sequences, in so far as it is decipherable at all, suggest no closer parallelism. (1951a, 164)

Childe then strongly differentiated his viewpoint from a parallelistic stance, proposing instead a model of convergent evolution in which cultures evolve to and from similar conditions through dissimilar steps. As Harris has noted, however, the dichotomy between the two viewpoints has perhaps been exaggerated, and here he emphasised that Morgan himself was not a strict parallelist but did in fact accept diffusion as one of the mechanisms by which the substantial uniformity of socio-cultural evolution was made possible (Harris 1968, 177–9).

Unlike the Boasian school in anthropology, Childe did not consider that the phenomenon of convergence invalidated the thesis of social evolution or indeed the analogy between social and organic evolution. And here he emphasised that in certain aspects the patterns of biological and social evolution were very similar.

> To Lamarck and Darwin 'evolution' described a process by which new species emerged – that is to say, a process of variation and differentiation. Organic evolution is never depicted pictorially by a bundle of parallel lines, but by a tree with branches all up the trunk and each branch bristling with twigs. In so far as the archaeological record could be represented by such a figure, it would disclose a process analogous to organic evolution. In fact, differentiation – the splitting of large homogeneous cultures into a multitude of distinct local cultures – is a conspicuous feature in the archaeological record. (1951a, 166)

Childe was aware, however, that it was convergence, i.e. the levelling up of distinct cultures by diffusion, which distinguished social from organic evolution. As noted previously Childe emphasised that diffusion was peculiar to social evolution. Cultural innovations, unlike organic mutations, could be transmitted from one generation to another, or from one society to another by non-biological mechanisms. In fact Childe defined diffusion as the adoption by one independent society of innovations initiated by another. (1951a, 179)

So in this respect Childe admitted that the analogy between the two processes broke down (1951a, 175). As Gathercole (1971) has emphasised, however, this is no cause to postulate a major crisis in Childe's thinking as Ravetz (1959) and Allen (1967) have done. To do this is to overlook the basic continuity in his argument from the thirties onwards. Childe had never denied that biological and social evolution differed in certain crucial aspects. Indeed from the thirties onwards he devoted considerable energy to clearly illustrating these differences. So the argument in *Social Evolution* is not new but rather a reaffirmation of long-held beliefs.

Furthermore, as Gathercole points out, far from denying the

usefulness of biological concepts in social evolution, Childe argued that,

> With certain modification the Darwinian formula of 'variation, heredity, adaptation and selection' can be transferred from organic to social evolution, and is even more intelligible in the latter domain than in the former.
> (1951a, 175)

Here Childe argued that the source of variation in social evolution, i.e. invention, was actually more comprehensible than its biological counterpart mutation.

> Not only does no one know the cause of the modification in the submicroscopic segment of a chromosome that produces a mutation, no one can predict when it will occur or in what direction. . . . But invention is something that everyone is doing every day – say in devising a substitute for a mislaid corkscrew or composing a really new sentence in an essay. (1951a, 175–6)

Similarly he argued that although the mechanism of social heredity was different from biological heredity it was nevertheless a familiar and intelligible process. 'It is effected by example and precept, by education, advertisement, and propaganda' (1951a, 176). Furthermore he emphasised that adaptation to the environment was as much a condition for the survival of societies as for organisms. Here however he stressed the importance of the social environment, both internal and external, to which a society adapts, arguing that this is much more variable than geography or climate.

Finally he pointed out that selection had operated in social evolution as it had in biological evolution.

> In the five hundred thousand years of humanity's existence an infinity of innovations must have been attempted or suggested. Owing to a rigorous process of selection, only a fraction have survived as being in the long run beneficial. (1951a, 177)

He warned that the term could only be applied to social evolution in a very limited sense, since the mechanisms of selection were very different from those operating in biological evolution.

> In the 'survival of the fittest' it is first those members of a population who carry the mutation who survive and multiply *at the expense of* those individuals who lack it. And then the new species thus established spreads by *elimi-*

nating other species. (1951a, 177)

While he accepted that similar selective mechanisms operate within and between societies he stressed the cumulative rather than the eliminative aspect of the historical process.

> Even in prehistory, when the change of culture in one region is so abrupt and drastic that we speak of one culture replacing another and infer the conquest of the region by a foreign society, most of the old achievements survive to be incorporated into the new culture. . . . At the same time the spread of invention is . . . not always, nor even usually, affected by competition between societies or cultures and the elimination of one or more competitors as independent entities. Diffusion generally means the adoption by one independent society of innovations initiated by another. But that again is a cumulative process.
>
> (1951a, 178–9)

In *Social Evolution*, then, Childe was using the archaeological record in a new and exciting fashion as a testing ground for social theory. Here it should be noted that he was in fact realising what many archaeologists today consider as a major objective for archaeology. It is now well known that in the late sixties and early seventies archaeologists began to reject what they considered as the historical objectives of archaeology, i.e. the reconstruction of the past, emphasising instead its function as a social science in contributing to the explanation of social behaviour (Trigger 1970). What is particularly interesting about Childe's work is that it embraced both these objectives. Unlike many 'new' archaeologists Childe did not set up a dichotomy between historical interpretation and social explanation, i.e. between history and the social sciences.

5

The Philosophical Background

One of the major points to emerge from the previous chapter was the importance of Childe's philosophical world-viewpoint in his assessment of historical models. It was seen that Childe had very strong beliefs in the nature of reality, which he characterised as a creative self-sufficient process with its own dynamic pattern. In denying a creator or a source of reality outside the historical process he placed himself firmly in a materialist, as opposed to an idealist, philosophical tradition.

Childe particularly emphasised the changeful nature of reality, and thus in these two fundamental aspects, i.e. nature's materialism and its changefulness, his world outlook coincided with a Marxist one. There were, however, important differences, for while Childe emphasised nature's changefulness he did not employ the Marxist explanation of change, i.e. dialectics. In fact he did not philosophise on the problem of change in any depth. Here, however, it is important to note that Childe's explicitly philosophical writings were not primarily concerned with the nature of reality. Rather this was assumed as self-evident. Indeed his only discussion of the topic was in the final chapter of his book *Society and Knowledge*, published in 1956.

Childe's philosophical works were for the most part concerned with the problem of knowledge. For Childe the interpretation of archaeological data raised epistemological questions. Archaeologists want to observe cultures, 'but the instrument of observation is itself culture. The results of observation must be expressed in the categories which we have inherited from our own society' (1949a, 5). Childe was thus very aware of the subjective nature of observation. Not only had man's way of looking at the world changed through time as his culture had changed, but his observation of that perception had also changed. In other words his knowledge of past knowledge had varied, depending on the conceptual model employed. For Childe the major problem in this context was thus one of interpretation. Aware of the relativity of world viewpoints he did not wish to interpret a past society's system of beliefs within an alien conceptual framework, i.e. according to the logic of the twentieth century. On the other hand, however, he did not consider the interpretation of a past society's thought within its own frame of reference to be a legitimate goal. Childe attempted to transcend this problem by his understanding of the nature of real knowledge, which he characterised as essentially practical. Here he made the interesting suggestion that the archaeological record, which in his eyes was the remains of the practical manifestation of knowledge, allowed the archaeologist to gain access to the society's objective knowledge rather than to its subjective world viewpoint.

Childe's argument had significant practical consequences for his approach to archaeology. Since he was concerned only with what he termed 'true knowledge' he felt no obligation to attempt to reconstruct past conceptual frameworks. Rather than try to interpret the fossilised behaviour patterns of extinct societies according to a hypothetical system of beliefs and thoughts, he was concerned only with what he termed their 'real historical function', i.e. their economic, social and scientific significance judged from a historical perspective.

As well as raising this question of subjectivity, Childe's excursion into philosophy brought to light an even more fundamental issue. Since he believed that knowledge had an essentially practical function to ensure the survival of the species, what then was the use of archaeology? In the end, however, Childe was unable to find any immediate practical value for the discipline. Nonetheless he did hope that archaeological knowledge would contribute to human understanding and thus help people to act more humanly (1956c, 127).

Childe published two articles specifically on the problem of knowledge: 'Social Worlds of Knowledge' (1949) and 'The Sociology of Knowledge' (1949). These were followed in 1956 by *Society and Knowledge* published for the World Perspective Series in which the 'most conscious and responsible minds' of the day outlined their basic philosophical understanding and beliefs (Anshen in 1956c, ix). Childe's philosophical thoughts, however, were not confined to these works and other publications to be taken into consideration include 'Magic, Craftsmanship and Science' (1950) and *Piecing Together the Past* (1956).

In 'Social Worlds of Knowledge' Childe examined the environment of man throughout history, both in terms of its content and extent, and in terms of man's perception of it. Here he made two main points. First, he argued that as we go back in history the environment in which man acts becomes smaller in extent and poorer in content:

> To any European society in the twentieth century the whole Earth is an effective element in the environment to be taken into account in planned activity. The most unlettered Englishman may send letters to New Zealand and eats meat from Argentina. To realise the shrinkage of this world in the past it suffices to look at a series of maps – a portulan of the fifteenth century, a reconstruction of Ptolemy's map a thousand years earlier, or of that of Hecataeus nearly a thousand years earlier still, and, finally, the extant copy of an Akkadian map of the late third millennium B.C. The latter was prepared by learned men of a literate and civilized people. . . . Yet it shows a tiny world, floating in a primeval ocean with Babylon at its centre. . . .
>
> Of course, as we go back, known worlds grow poorer in content as well as smaller in extent. Plainly we must gradually drain off the discoveries of modern science. . . . To recapture the environment of a past society we must, then, divest it of many of the physical, chemical, biological and geological properties that we should find in it.
> (1949a, 10–12)

Secondly, he held that man's way of perceiving his environment had changed through time. Here Childe argued that the environment to which a society adjusts is a world of ideas, collective representations that differ not only in extent and content, but also in structure. Childe's basic premise in this paper was that thought is patterned by fundamental intellectual constructs which he termed 'categories of knowledge' after Durkheim. His main argument was that these categories are neither timeless nor *a priori* but change with changes in society, and to illustrate this point he showed how the concepts of number and space have evolved through time.

Similarly Childe emphasised that the 'laws of logic' were likewise not immutable but had changed throughout history.

> Levy-Bruhl, you remember, styles natives' thinking 'prelogical'. . . . Primitive thinking does not conform to the

rules formulated by Aristotle. Nor did the thinking of the ancient Egyptians and Sumerians. In his masterly study of the oldest extant results of speculative thinking about Nature, Frankfort can quote text and text where, in the 'mythopoeic thought' of the Bronze Age civilizations of the Orient, the principles of identity and non-contradiction seem to be ignored, while space and causality are employed very differently from the usage of Newton or Kant. (1949a, 17)

Childe was thus highly aware of the subjective element in observation, of the very important interaction between the observer and what is observed. The way of observing necessarily affects the observer's knowledge of what is observed. Here Childe gave the example of the approach to primitive, and to early civilised man employed by nineteenth-century ethnographers who imposed a nineteenth-century world outlook upon the thought-patterns of people with very different ways of thinking.

All have cheerfully assumed that contemporary savages, the Sumerians, the Egyptians, the Ionians, started out, as modern science tries to with mind and matter, subject and object, neatly and rigidly separated. They have then to assume that these societies erroneously put back into the object elements proper to the subject – personifying natural phenomena, peopling nature with ghosts, spirits and gods, infusing her with *mana*, and gratuitously postulating personal beings to push and pull what really is an automatic machine! We know now where they went wrong. Having first killed the culture they wanted to study as an object, they dissected and disarticulated its corpse and then tried to re-animate isolated members with equally isolated infusions from their own living culture. (1949a, 23–4)

The important problem for Childe was thus to find a way out of the subjective limitations of cultural background. It was, in his eyes, essential to avoid imposing a modern conceptual framework upon primitive or prehistoric outlooks. He did not, however, as stated previously, consider the interpretation of a culture within its own frame of reference as a possible goal.

'All history' wrote Collingwood, 'is the re-enactment of past thought in the historian's own mind', and, more explicitly, 'The historian re-enacts, in his own mind the thoughts and motives of the agent'. But that too, is impossible. Empirically – to take what should be an easy case – I cannot 're-enact in my mind' Pythagoras' thoughts and motives' when he 'discovered' his theorem; . . . I can follow his proof. But that does not make me rush off to sacrifice an ox. Still less can I guess why Babylonian clerks a thousand years before Pythagoras covered hundreds of tablets with problems laboriously devised to illustrate the theorem. . . . But theoretically, too, the task is impossible. Collingwood tells me in effect to empty my head of all the ideas, categories, and values derived from my society in order to fill it with those of an extinct society. But that is doubly impossible. On the one hand the drainage process would not leave a *tabula rasa*, but nothing at all. . . . On the other hand, there would be nothing to put into that nothing, since collective representations exist only for societies, and would be extinguished with the extinction of the society for which they existed. (1949a, 24–5)

In 'Magic, Craftsmanship and Science', published in 1950, Childe again emphasised this point.

Now the late R. G. Collingwood asserted that a historian must 're-enact in his own mind the thoughts and motives of the agent'. Let me say at once that I do not believe that rethinking dead men's thoughts is the business of the historian at all. I do not believe it is really possible even with written documents to disclose the deceased's avowed intentions. Without such clues it is plainly hopeless to try and recapture the precise emotions and hopes that inspired, for instance, the builders of Stonehenge. (1950c, 1)

Childe did, however, consider that he had a way out of the subjectivity dilemma based on what he regarded as the nature of 'real' or 'true' thought.

In practice the separation of subject from object is transcended. Real thoughts of the past have issued in action. Real thinking has already been objectified. To study a past society there is no need to turn its real thoughts into objects, for that has already been done. The relics and monuments studied by archaeology are patently objects, and need no translation into an alien conceptual framework. (1949a, 25)

Here, he rested his argument on the practical nature of real thought on the following passage from Collingwood,

Purely theoretical thinking is not real thinking and does not lead to real knowing. . . . Real thinking is always to some extent experimental in its method. It starts from practice and returns to practice. (1949a, 25)

In 'Magic, Craftsmanship and Science' Childe went on to devote considerable attention to the important question of the relationship between real or true knowledge and false knowledge. Characterising magic as false knowledge and science as true knowledge, he defined the latter as 'those simple truths of which men in all ages possessed a store' (1950c, 5) from J. Frazer's *The Magic Art* (1925). It is perhaps surprising that he did not attempt a more concrete definition of the term considering the important role it plays in his approach to the interpretation of archaeological remains. He does, however, supplement it in a footnote by two passages, the first from Malinowski, the second from Collingwood.

If by Science be understood a body of rules and conceptions, based on experience and derived from it by logical inference, embodied in material achievements and carried on by some sort of social organization – then even the lowest savages have the beginnings of science. . . .

The sort of natural science which is inseparable from an intelligent exploitation of the natural world, means watching and remembering and handing down from father to son things which it is useful to know. (1950c, 5)

Magic he attempted to define behaviourally rather than psychologically since in these terms it could be subject to empirical study while in the latter terms it could not.

Confine the term to those activities in which the practitioner claims to be utilizing forces different in kind from those recognised as normal and necessary in everyday life – by the common sense of his society. Then the prehistoric archaeologist will be silenced, as motives and beliefs lie outside his purview. But in practice such a subjective criterion is hard to apply even in ethnography, or, for that matter, in a study of English coal miners or medical practitioners. For instance, Mr. T. E. Williams, who himself studied under Malinowski and who confesses a predilection for psychological interpretations, finds the borderline between magic and common sense (i.e. science) elusive. The 'medicines', *wen*, administered to their gardens by his *Keraki* can have only a magical utility. 'Yet it may be,' he writes, 'that in native estimation their use is almost as much a matter of common sense, as, say, erecting a pole to support the yam vine.' Such an ambiguous criterion has plainly no part in a scientific definition. It is safer to follow behaviourist lines and to reply on the overt act than its alleged motive. Frazer has amply illustrated the appropriate behaviour patterns. So, whenever we observe people systematically performing acts that in the light of modern knowledge have proved futile and irrelevant to their manifest purpose but which conform to the pattern he has defined, let us frankly call them magical. (1950c, 9–10)

Childe makes two main points in this paper. First he argues that there is no rigid separation between scientific and magical activities – more specifically that magical activities supplement science. This is primarily directed against Malinowski's thesis that science and magic differ in subject matter, mental process, social organisation and pragmatic function (1950c, 4).

Secondly he shows with reference to archaeological research that magic has a long history stretching back to the Old Stone Age, thus disproving the 'Fall of Man' thesis of the *Kulturhistorische Schule* where magical practices are viewed as perverse innovations accumulated by societies that not only failed to evolve but have actually degenerated.

Accordingly, as far as archaeological evidence goes, magical practices are as old as *Homo Sapiens* or even older, magical procedures were habitually invoked to supplement the conspicuously efficient skill and material equipment of the earliest hunters whose lives are really known to us, craft tools were invested with magical power in the New Stone Age, when competent flint-miners resorted to magical rites and surgeons acted on the familiar magical theory of disease, and the oldest relevant documents left by our cultural ancestors show the applications of science in craftsmanship hedged about with magical precautions. In other words the available archaeological evidence, exiguous though it inevitably be, suffices to indicate that a belief in magic has been a 'universal faith' in a temporal as well as a spatial sense. There is not a scrap of evidence to sugest that it was a cancerous growth that at a late stage and among constitutionally inferior races obstructed the natural current of rational science. (1950c, 17)

As in 'Social Worlds of Knowledge' Childe emphasised that the prehistorian should not aim to recreate the magical practices and motives of past societies.

Accordingly the prehistorian of science must renounce any pretension of re-enacting in his own mind the thoughts and motives of its pre-literate pioneers; for the precise rites, spells and taboos that accompanied their successful activities cannot be revived. There is at any time a finite – and generally quite modest – number of ways of attaining any attainable result. The number of imaginable ways of attaining the unattainable, is literally infinite. . . . Secondly the practice of magic is the outcome and expression of a distinctive pattern of thought or logic. Our preliterate precursors were thinking thoughts that we cannot recapture not so much because they would be expressed in an untranslatable language, in a system of conventional symbols the meanings of which have perished with the society that sanctioned and maintained the conventions. They are unthinkable rather because they conformed to a totally alien logic. (1950c, 17–18)

Similarly in *Piecing Together the Past*, his most detailed analysis of archaeological methodology, published in 1956, Childe again stressed this point, this time even more forcibly. Indeed he gives the example of the manufacture of a Mousterian scraper to illustrate that our lack of knowledge of the total manufacturing process is in fact advantageous in that it highlights and separates the real knowledge of the manufacturer from the illusionary aspects. Childe imagined the total process to be something as follows,

To make a D-scraper, collect a flint nodule (1) at full moon, (2) after fasting all day, (3) address him politely with 'words of power', (4) . . . strike him thus with a hammerstone, (5) smeared with the blood of a sacrificed mouse. (1956a, 171)

And in this context he emphasised that,

Technical and scientific progress has of course just been discovering that (1), (2), (3) and (5) are quite irrelevant to the success of the operation prescribed in (4). These acts were . . . futile accessories, expressive of ideological delusions. It is just these that have been erased from the archaeological record. Errors expunged, knowledge stands out all the clearer to be re-known. (1956a, 171–2)

Thus it would seem that for Childe the fact that the archaeological record was limited to the material remains of past societies was in some ways a blessing in disguise, allowing for a clear interpretation of a past society's 'true' as opposed to 'false' knowledge. Here it should be noted that this lack of interest in the subjective world-viewpoint of past societies can be traced back to a classic Marxist source. Indeed it was Marx himself who emphasised that just as one does not evaluate an individual in terms of what he thinks of himself, so one does not judge a period in history in terms of its own consciousness (Bottomore and Rubel 1956, 52). The strength of Childe's commitment to this viewpoint, however, was not typical of his Marxist contemporaries. As Gathercole has pointed out, at that time notable Marxists were explicitly expressing the hope of reconstructing the past thoughts and beliefs of former societies (1971, 230).

In 'The Sociology of Knowledge' published in 1949, Childe begins with a discussion of the relationship between mind and matter, subject and object. Here he pointed out that this was a distinction learnt only in a relatively recent part of man's evolution. In the Oriental Bronze Age for example, the subject/object dichotomy was not clearly differentiated. Childe termed this type of world outlook mythological. It was not until the separation between subject and object was made explicit that knowledge became a problem. How could the subject know the object?

In this context Childe discussed very briefly the epistemological basis to empiricism, idealism and dialectical materialism. As in 'Social Worlds of Knowledge' he rejected a passive role to the mind as only reflecting external reality. While he emphasised the active role of mind in patterning external reality he differentiated himself from an idealist in that he did not believe that (1) man's fundamental intellectual constructs, i.e. the categories of knowledge, were innate, and (2) the mind created the categories and their contents.

Childe attributed to Marx the discovery that the categories are neither absolute nor eternal but are conditioned by the productive forces used by society and must change with the appropriate relations of production. He warned, however, that philosophers and natural scientists had been disregarding this finding.

Academic philosophers naturally ignored a discovery that

would disturb the tranquility of their ivory towers. Natural
scientists in the meantime were content to go on transcending the subject-object opposition in practice, unworried
by epistemological or metaphysical puzzles, till they realised quite recently that their empirical data just will not
fit into the categories of Aristotelian logic and that observation alters the object observed. (1949c, 303)

Anthropologists, on the other hand, in particular Emile Durkheim, had already become aware of the relativity of knowledge.

Logic presents different characters at different periods of
history; it develops like societies themselves. . . . Its laws,
far from being graven from all eternity on the mental
constitutions of men, depend upon factors that are historical and consequently social.

(Durkheim in Childe 1949c, 305)

Childe's primary aim in this paper was to show that Durkheim's epistemology had several important points of agreement with Marxist philosophy; first as concerns the practical
function of knowledge, secondly as regards the social structure
of knowledge and thirdly with respect to the social content of
knowledge. While Childe upheld all of these three points, it is
significant that he disagreed with Durkheim's thesis concerning
the origin of the categories of knowledge. Very briefly, he
considered these to be ultimately based on the technological
component of society rather than, as Durkheim had suggested,
on society itself.

What Durkheim overlooked was that no people can survive at all without some rudiments of practical techniques –
for securing food, producing fire, fashioning tools and so
on. And after all even an infant can begin to change its
environment directly, by appropriate actions of its own.
At first, no doubt these actions would be accompanied by
irrelevant symbolic gestures or noises. In primitive
societies the effective manipulations of hunting, fire-kind-
ling and tool-making are certainly mixed up with symbolic
actions and magical practices. But with the gradual growth
of technical skills, successful craft practices began to infect
society's view of nature. The decisive contributions of the
'natural philosophers' of ancient Iona, as Farrington's recent book so brilliantly explains, was that they tried, for
the first time as far as we know, to construct a model of

nature based on the successful operations of the crafts.
They at least started the search for a method of explanation, a model of reality based on the analogy of processes
completely under social control and therefore intelligible.
While the muscular energy of men, cattle and donkeys
were the only motive-power regularly controlled by society, the search could not reach a satisfactory model. It is
water-power, steam and electricity that have made a completely depersonalised model of nature conceivable.
(1949c, 307–8)

In specifying the technological component as the main determining influence on the ideology, Childe was of course showing
a strong Marxist bias. However, leaving no doubt as to his
theoretical stance, he reserved the concluding paragraphs in
the paper for a staunch defence of Marxist philosophy.

First Childe emphasised that it was Marx who had initially
discovered the distorting effect of ideology (used in the negative sense as false dogma) on a society's world outlook. And
here he suggested that Marxism had banished both classical
economics and Hegelian metaphysics to the domain of
ideology. He was aware, however, that Marxist critics had
taken this as a refutation of Marxism itself, seeing the latter
also as an ideology which distorts reality. Childe strongly disagreed with this viewpoint, arguing that Marxism was a scientific system which was conscious of this danger and expressly
guarding against it. Unfortunately however, Childe did not
specify in what way Marxism overcomes this problem and thus
does not adequately answer this very important criticism.
Nevertheless he had to admit that Marxism like other world
outlooks was relative and socially determined. Here he argued
that the sociological limits of knowledge can be transcended
only in so far as to guide the next step in practice and in this
context he finished on a fitting revolutionary note, 'We need
not predict what will happen thereafter when ideological dis-
tortions have been eliminated by the abolition of classes with
class interests' (1949c, 309).

In *Society and Knowledge* (1956) Childe presented his final
and most comprehensive analysis of his theory of knowledge.
Here his entire approach is founded upon two basic premises,
which even he himself seems to have considered as controver-
sial at least in some circles.

To deserve the name, I contend, knowledge must be communicable and in that sense public and also useful, I mean capable of being translated into successful action. The first qualification may come as a shock to mystics, whether religious or not. The second would certainly scandalise a Greek of the age of Plato and Aristotle and many academic scientists today who follow them in the pursuit of 'science for its own sake'. (1956c, 4)

Childe differentiated knowledge as 'communicable' first from stimulus-response which is transmitted biologically and secondly from memory which he argued was similarly instinctual being a strictly private experience analogous to conditioned responses. Childe thus imposed very important limitations on the nature of what he regarded as 'communicable' restricting the term to communication on a symbolic level only. Indeed he further limits communication to only certain types of symbolic vehicles, primarily language and mathematics.

Other kinds of symbols may convey and express ideas but knowledge as here defined does not find expression in the symbols of art or religion any more than in dreams, the private symbols of the Unconscious (a mythical entity imagined but successfully used by psychoanalysts). (1956c, 67)

Childe deduced the practical utility of knowledge from what he considered to be its historical and biological function as a mechanism to ensure the survival of *Homo sapiens*.

Homo sapiens seems to be literally omnivorous. No innate appetite guides a weaned child what to eat as it impels a calf to eat grass. Many poisons look eminently appetizing. If men had to learn their avoidance by trial and error, human mortality would have been so heavy that the species would hardly have multiplied. Just as organisms with several reflex responses have managed better to survive and multiply more economically than those more scantily equipped, just as animals that learn by experience are still better fitted to survive and reproduce their kind, so men, who can learn from one another's experiences have been the most successful species biologically. If then we say that historically the biological function of knowledge has been to ensure the survival and multiplication of Homo sapiens, we are not in fact importing into biology an extraneous teleological idea any more than we say the same of the clam's shadow-closure reflex or the rat's capacity to learn by experience. Biologically all mechanisms for controlling and directing any organism's behaviour in accordance with environmental conditions have proved their utility, and have themselves survived, by enabling their possessors to survive and multiply. Communicable knowledge is just the latest in time and the most successful of such mechanisms. Who can then deny that knowledge is useful at least biologically? (1956c, 8–9)

Childe's definition of knowledge as 'an ideal reproduction of the world serviceable for co-operative action thereon' (1956c, 54) is essentially a confirmation of his argument concerning the practical function of knowledge. The term 'co-operative' in this context is interesting, for at first sight it would seem to differentiate his view of knowledge from that of both Marx and Durkheim, neither of whom made this qualification. Childe used the term, however, in an extremely loose sense, extending its meaning to cover all social activities, even war. In fact, he used it as synonomous with social in the sense of pertaining to society. Unless this peculiarly Childean usage is kept in mind it is easy to misinterpret the basic points in his argument.

Childe chose the term 'reproduction' as opposed to 'reflection' in his definition of knowledge in order to highlight the activity of the observer in the act of observation.

> Re*production* is used to emphasise that knowers do not just receive impressions and passively reflect them as mirrors do. They produce a pattern from them. (1956c, 54)

As in his previous papers, he argued that the outlines of this pattern were formed by basic conceptual constructs which Durkheim had termed categories.

> A *category* connotes the outline of a pattern, the kind of relation holding between elements in a pattern that is itself presumed to be a component pattern of the external world. It is not perhaps under this title that categories are familiar to every reader – I mean 'space', 'time', 'causality', 'substance', and so on. Each denotes a way in which empirical data are supposed to hang together to form a pattern and the kind of pattern thus formed. (1956c, 73)

Childe's discussion of the categories in *Society and Knowledge* followed similar lines of thought to that presented in both 'Social Worlds of Knowledge' and 'The Sociology of Knowledge'. As before he emphasised their social nature, stressing that they were both derived from society and that they changed with changes in society. Likewise he insisted on the relativity of truth which he defined as the correspondence between the conceptual model of reality and reality itself.

> Each society may erect its own proper and distinctive reproduction of the external world, and the several reproductions or worlds of knowledge may differ in structure as well as in content since the categories have been shown to be neither so universal nor so eternal as older philosophies pretended. There thus may be, and indeed are and have been, many divergent and even contrasted conceptual worlds expressed in equally disparate systems of propositions or 'truths'. That is why there must be degrees of truth. For the several ideal reproductions of reality cannot all correspond equally closely to that reality. (1956c, 108)

Furthermore he re-emphasised his argument on the practical nature of verification.

> There can only be one *test* of truth as thus defined, only one criterion by which to decide whether a conceptual reproduction does in fact correspond to the external world. That is action. For we have insisted from the beginning that the function of knowledge is practical, it is to furnish a guide to action. From the propositions that express it, can be deduced practically serviceable rules for behaviour. The success of action, guided by the rules thus deduced is the decisive test of the proposition from which they are derived. (1956c, 107)

Here it should be noted that this emphasis on practice as the test of truth is a classic Marxist argument, once more illustrating Childe's debt to this materialist philosophy.

> The question whether human thinking can pretend to objective truth is not a theoretical but a *practical* question. Man must prove the truth, i.e. the reality and the power of the 'this sideness' of his thinking in practice. The dispute of the reality or the non-reality of thinking that is isolated from practice is a purely *scholastic* question.
>
> (Marx 1845 in Bottomore and Rubel 1956, 67)

In the final chapter of *Society and Knowledge* Childe gave an interesting insight into his personal beliefs. In its essence he saw reality as a changeful creative process which is neither teleological nor cyclical.

> Reality is an activity, a process that is neither repeating

itself over and over again nor yet is approximating to a predetermined goal or the realization of a preconceived plan. It is on the contrary genuinely creative, constantly bringing forth what has never been produced before, genuine novelties.

I could indeed adduce arguments in support of this thesis. Half a million years of human history show not only some repetitions, but much more the repeated emergence of novel inventions, unprecedented patterns of behaviour and of social organization, fresh needs, desires and aspirations, in a word new values. In natural history 'natural selection' is 'a mechanism for generating an exceedingly high degree of improbability'. (1956c, 123)

At the same time, however, he did not see it as a wholly unpredictable process.

That is not to deny any pattern, any order to Reality, or to suggest that the pattern that will unfold is arbitrary, capricious and unrelated to the knowable realized pattern expressed in History. On the contrary it must be a continuation and development of the existing pattern, already realized and knowable, and therefore determined by the latter in general but not in detail. Creation is not a making something out of nothing, but refashioning what already is. (1956c, 124)

For Childe, then, the pattern of reality was incomplete and created itself in a developmental process through time.

Furthermore, in his eyes, there was nothing outside this process, whether this be conceived in terms of God or the Absolute. And in denying transcendence he had thus to deny the cognitive value of transcendental experiences.

I must deny the revelation in religious experience, whatever that may be, of any Reality transcending the process. That is not to deny all value to such experience, but only cognitive value – truth. (1956c, 130)

At its lowest he viewed religion as an assurance which enabled men to participate in Reality, at its highest as the originator of new ideals of the Good and the Beauty. However, because these ideals were imagined he denied any eternal or absolute value to them.

As stated previously, Childe considered knowledge to have an essentially practical function. He did not, however, believe that the pursuit of knowledge for its own sake was futile or meaningless. Indeed he seemed to regard this type of activity as an important source for discoveries of great practical utility. As regards his own role in society he wrote the following,

> I am an archaeologist and devote my time to trying to gather information about the behaviour of men long since dead. I like doing this and my society pays me quite well for doing it. Yet neither I nor society can see any immediate practical applications for the information I gather; we are indeed quite sure that it will not increase the production of bombs nor butter. Still, we like to think that even archaeological knowledge may someday prove useful to some society. Indeed I might even venture to hope that the archaeological knowledge embodied in the present book may be useful in helping readers to think more clearly and so to behave more humanly. (1956c, 127)

Childe thus saw himself as essentially a producer of knowledge, and although aware of his own mortality, there is a hint that he hoped to attain immortality of a kind through the acceptance and propagation of his knowledge by society.

> Society is immortal, but its members are born and die. Hence any idea accepted by Society and objectified is likewise immortal. In creating ideas that are accepted, any mortal member of Society attains immortality – yes, though his name be forgotten as his bodily form dissolve. Personally I desire no more. (1956c, 130)

6

Childe and Marxism

As Daniel pointed out the most important single problem of Childe's lifework concerns his debt to Marxism.

> The great puzzle of Childe at all times was to what extent
> he was a Marxist (or a Marrist) and to what extent he paid
> lip-service to an Outsider philosophy? (Daniel 1958, 66)

In this book references to Marxism have been numerous and it is clear that it must be considered as a major intellectual force in Childe's thought. The manner and degree to which Marxism influenced his work as a whole, however, cannot be fully appreciated without an outline of the basic issues involved in Marxist theory.

Here the first point to be stressed is that Marxism as such is not a homogeneous doctrine but has undergone many interpretations and revisions during the course of its development (Jordan 1967). In its broadest sense it refers to the system of thought founded on the work of Karl Marx (1818–83) and his collaborator Friedrich Engels (1820–95) characterised by an economic interpretation of society and a materialist philosophical world outlook. Very briefly, Marx's principle of social analysis comprises a division of society into three major components, economy, sociology and ideology. Of these the economy is regarded as fundamental and as providing an explanation for the form taken by the sociology and ideology. Here it should be noted that the economy, or in Marxist terminology 'the mode of production of material life', is further subdivided into the 'productive forces', i.e. the technology together with the skill required to work it, and the 'relations of production', i.e. the social relations under which the technology operates. For Marx the major motivating source of historical change was the contradiction between the productive forces and the relations of production. Here, he argued that while the productive forces are constantly developing owing to new inventions, the relations of production at any given period are comparatively fixed and resist change. It is thus that the relations of production which begin by 'expressing' (i.e. serving) the needs of the development of the forces of production, end by becoming the 'fetters' upon this development. Marx held that as science and technology progress the relations of production have to change in order to meet the demands of the new technology. Thus commences the 'period of social revolution' when 'the entire immense superstructure is more or less rapidly transformed' (Marx in Bottomore and Rubel 1956, 52).

In sociological terms this was seen as a struggle between the exploiters and the exploited. The concept of class is central to historical materialism (Bottomore 1973, 19). Very briefly Marx held that each major economic structure or system brings into being its own division of society into economic classes with opposing interests.

> The history of all hitherto existing society is the history of class struggles. Freeman and slave, patrician and plebeian, lord and serf, guild-master and journeyman, in a word oppressor and oppressed, stood in constant opposition to one another, carried on an uninterrupted, now hidden, now open fight, a fight that each time ended either in a revolutionary reconstitution of society at large, or in the common ruin of the contending classes.
> (Marx in Bottomore and Rubel 1956, 207)

Both Marx and Engels warned against the mechanical application of their approach; the superstructure could and does influence the economic base.

> According to the materialist conception of history, the determining element in history is *ultimately* the production and reproduction in real life. More than this Marx nor I have ever asserted.
>
> If therefore someone twists this into the statement that the economic element is the *only* determining one, he transforms it into a meaningless abstract and absurd phrase. The economic situation is the basis, but the various elements of the superstructure – political forms of the class struggle and its consequences, constitutions established by the victorious class after successful battle, etc. – forms of law – and then even the reflexes of all these actual struggles in the brains of the combatants: political, legal and philosophical theories, religious ideas and their further development into systems of dogma – also exercise

their influence upon the course of historical struggles and in many cases preponderate in determining their *form*. (Engels in Harris 1968, 244–5)

In the historical materialism of the Soviet school Marx's approach has been systematically developed and embedded in a system of universal world processes that is held to constitute the materialist dialectics. The latter, it is claimed, provide a general explanation of the 'driving forces' behind movement and development in the world, the source of all change being the contradiction inherent in all things. Dialectics is in essence the Hegelian formula of thesis, anti-thesis and synthesis applied to all levels of phenomena. Dialectical materialism, or in Engels terminology 'modern materialism', accepted both the principle of evolution and the principle of sudden leaps to which gradual change necessarily leads. In *Anti-Duhring* (1888) Engels formulated three laws of the dialectic, the law of the impenetration of opposites, the law of transition from quantity into quality and the law of the negation of the negation, the third law being a restatement of the Hegelian triad (Jordan 1967, 167–82).

It is well known that Marx's major concern was an analysis of contemporary capitalism and his writings on pre-capitalist society play a comparatively minor role in his work as a whole. In the *Preface* to *The Critique of Political Economy* and in more detail in the *Formen*, Marx distinguished four major epochs in world history, i.e. the Asiatic, the Ancient, the Feudal and the modern Bourgeois, the latter being the last antagonistic form of society (Hobsbawm 1964). Out of capitalism, Marx predicted the rise of a new type of society in which economic classes were destroyed and class conflict finally resolved. Furthermore it was to be a time when man realised his true humanity and lived in harmony with himself and with nature.

> Communism as complete naturalism is humanism and as complete humanism is naturalism. It is the *definitive* resolution of the antagonism between man and Nature, and between man and man. It is the true solution of the conflict between existence and essence, between objectification and self-affirmation, between freedom and necessity, between individual and species. It is the solution of the riddle of history and knows itself to be this solution.
> (Marx in Bottomore and Rubel 1956, 244)

Marx's belief in the general progressive nature of history

links his thought to that of Darwin, Morgan, Spencer and Tylor as well as to a common heritage of eighteenth-century doctrine. As Harris had remarked, its only distinction lies in the strength of its apocalyptic emphasis (1968, 222).

From his anthropological notebooks it is now known that Marx had a fairly broad knowledge of ethnology and towards the end of his life was working on a materialist analysis of primitive society based on the work of the American Lewis Morgan. Marx, however, never lived to complete the task, which was finished by Engels in *The Origin of the Family* published in 1884. This text, together with Morgan's *Ancient Society* (1877), was to become the main theoretical source for Soviet archaeology until well into the present century (Tolstoy 1952, 8–17).

It is interesting that at the time of Childe's visit to the U.S.S.R. in 1934, Soviet archaeology was undergoing a major theoretical upheaval in order to align it with official Marxist theory (Miller 1956). Archaeology as it had existed prior to 1930 was replaced by the history of pre-capitalist societies. At the basis of the new discipline was the idea that archaeological remains are not to be studied for their own sake but are only sources for understanding and reconstructing the society which produced them. Accordingly, the ultimate aim of archaeology was to reconstruct the forms and stages of society prior to capitalism. After extensive study and discussion the orthodox developmental scheme of world stages was given as follows. This, as Childe pointed out was a classification based on the 'relations of production' (1944b, 23).

I   *Pre-class society* (a) the formation of human society; (b) pre-clan era; (c) clan (rodovoye) matriarchal society; (d) clan patriarchal society; (e) stage of decomposition of the clan (transition from the clan to the village community).

II *Class society, slave holding formation* (a) oriental, primitive slave-holding society; (b) developed, ancient slave-holding society.

III *Feudal society* (a) early feudalism; (b) developed or later feudalism.

IV *Capitalist society*

V   *Classless society* (a) socialism; (b) communism. Communist society is the final stage of development and is not subject to further changes. (Miller 1956, 78–9)

At the same time Soviet archaeology took a firmly evolutionist standpoint and the formation of the Russian and European peoples was seen as a spontaneous and autochthonous stage-by-stage process. This it should be noted was principally directed against the Indo-European and racist theories propagated in the West. Diffusion and migration were rejected as bourgeois concepts and the expression 'the great migration of peoples' was prohibited and dropped from use (Miller 1956, 80).

It is interesting to note that 1934 was also important for Soviet archaeology in that it marked the death of N. Y. Marr, one of Russia's most prominent post-revolutionary archaeologists. Like Childe, Marr had strong philological interests, his major concern being the development of the Indo-European language family. Here his most notable contribution was to abandon the western hypothesis of an original Indo-European mother tongue, replacing this by a new linguistic thesis – the Japhetic theory. Basically this asserted that the development of the Indo-European languages was not divergence from a common source but rather convergence from a multifarious linguistic base, i.e. the Japhetic languages of the Mediterranean basin. In this context Marr attempted to apply Marxism to linguistic theory by viewing language as part of the superstructure and relating changes in this sphere to changes in the mode of production. In archaeology the main effect of Marr's theory was to intensify the narrow evolutionist framework adhered to by the orthodox school. Marr's thought was very influential in Soviet archaeology for almost thirty years until 1950 when it was finally denounced by Stalin as a gross vulgarisation and perversion of Marxism (Ellis and Davis 1951, 243ff.).

Marxism, however, is not solely a set of beliefs but has a strong practical component which takes the form of political activism. It was Marx himself who insisted on the unity of theory and practice. 'The philosophers have only *interpreted* the world in various ways, the point is to *change* it' (Marx in Bottomore and Rubel 1956, 69).

In effect, then, to be a Marxist usually implies some commitment to left wing or communist politics as well as subscribing a certain type of social and philosophical analysis. Although in this book we are primarily concerned with the theoretical aspects of Marxism, it is important to note that Childe himself did not limit his Marxism in this way. As Green has shown, in addition to his direct participation in Australian politics, throughout his thirty-five years in Britain, Childe kept in close contact with left-wing movements and his commitment to the communist cause was never doubted by his friends within the party (Green 1976, 30ff.).

Because of the close relationship between Marxist theory and practice, a discussion of Childe's Marxism which does not examine his politics is no doubt a limited one. Yet it is outside the framework of the present work to analyse either his political activities or beliefs. No doubt this would be an interesting line of research, but it belongs to the domain of the biographer or modern historian, rather than the prehistorian. What will be discussed, however, is Childe's attitude towards Soviet scholarship, in particular archaeology, for this is of course very relevant to his own work as an archaeologist.

The first point to stress in this context is that Childe did not begin his work in European prehistory with a Marxist interpretation of the past. As he himself admitted in 'Retrospect', his initial view of European prehistory was essentially 'a pre-literate substitute for the conventional politico-military history with cultures, instead of statesmen, as actors, and migrations in place of battles' (1958a, 70). What Childe did not admit in 'Retrospect', however, was the extent to which his thinking at this time diverged from Marxism. In fact his initial explanation of progress in Europe with its emphasis on intellectual development as a primary causative factor of culture change could be regarded as the very antithesis of historical materialism. While a Marxist would seek the explanation for man's intellectual development in his technological, economic and social evolution, Childe saw in the former an explanation for the latter. It was, of course, the close correlation that Childe postulated between linguistic and intellectual development which led him to view the Aryan-speaking peoples as the dominant progressive force in European prehistory and as the founders of modern civilisation.

In 'Retrospect' Childe traced the beginnings of his economic approach to *The Bronze Age* published in 1930, where he argued that the use of bronze implied both regular trade and the social division of labour (1958a, 71). It was not until 1935, however, that he further developed this line of approach, and in 'Changing Methods and Aims in Prehistory' he extended his economic analysis of the Bronze Age to cover the Stone and

Iron Ages. The result was a novel interpretation of the three ages as economic stages initiated by important economic revolutions.

In the previous year Childe had visited the U.S.S.R. for the first time and as well as visiting museums in Leningrad and Moscow (1935d), he acquired some knowledge of Soviet archaeological theory. As noted above, at that time the Soviet view of the past was dominated by a strong evolutionary thesis based on Engels's interpretation of Morgan, the main prehistoric model being the sociological one outlined on page 153. Childe, however, did not approve of the Russian periodisation of world history based on the 'relations of production'. While he understood the reasoning behind the adoption of this scheme and admitted the importance of social structure in influencing technological development, in his eyes it was not suitable for archaeological classification.

> The mere knowledge of bronze, the smith's presence alone, did not of itself produce even new tool types, nor enlarge social productivity by saws, wheeled vehicles or metal sickles. Iron of itself does not draw men on to fresh devices. . . . In other words as Stalin puts it 'the relations of production constitute just as essential an element in production as the productive forces of society' – its tools and the traditional skill of the operatives. . . .
>
> For this reason a classification based on the property relations within which tools were used might be more significant (than a technological model). Soviet archaeologists have in fact tried to build up a system on this basis speaking of a 'pre-clan stage', a 'stage of the matriarchal clan' and so on. However sound this may be in theory the trouble is that the archaeological record is, to put it mildly, vague as to the social organization of preliterate communities. The scheme would therefore lack one essential qualification for a scientific classification. (1944b, 23)

Here Childe suggested that the technological model was in fact more helpful than its sociological counterpart to a Marxist view of the past, arguing that it illuminated the contradictions in the economy central to the Marxist view of change.

> Indeed it might be claimed as a justification for the traditional system that it does permit us to detect just those contradictions between the material forces of production and the relations of production on which Marxism lays

such stress. (1944b, 23)

Childe's functional-economic interpretation of the three-age model, however, radically altered his view of its role in the discipline. No longer was it seen as a chronological framework but rather as an index of what he termed 'human progress'. In other words like the Soviet model it demarcated socio-economic stages in world history. Unlike the latter, however, it was not conceived in narrow evolutionist terms. Childe did not follow the Russian example and abandon diffusion as an important mechanism of change.

> A pseudo-Marxist materialism might indeed represent the stages of progress, the archaeological 'ages' as mere adjustment evoked by the environment independently, though not simultaneously, in various regions. But no sane prehistorian will contend that the strandloopers who have left the kitchen middens in Denmark began of their own initiative to cultivate emmer or to tame sheep. For no wild wheat grew in Denmark to cultivate and no wild sheep ranged the forests for the strandloopers to tame. The distinctive elements of Danish neolithic cultures – the plants cultivated and the animals bred therein – can only have reached the Baltic by some sort of diffusion.
> (1935c, 12)

In the 1939 edition of *The Dawn*, Childe thus considered that he had been paying lip service to Marxism. For while he adopted the Marxist structural analysis of society in his descriptions of cultures, 'first the food quest, then secondary industries and trade, only thereafter social and religious institutions' (1958a, 72), he did not adopt the current orthodox evolutionist view of socio-cultural change.

It should be remembered, however, that in the Orient Childe had not restricted his employment of Marxist theory in this way. Here he explained culture change without reference to external events as an evolutionary process in which society developed through three major socio-economic stages, food-gathering savagery, food-producing barbarism and civilisation. Furthermore, in the context of Scottish prehistory Childe had explicitly experimented with the Marrist evolutionary model and indeed believed that this gave a more satisfactory picture of the development of Scottish culture than the current diffusionist model (1946a). Nevertheless he did not fully endorse the Soviet theory but had to admit migrations and the impact of foreign cultures. 'The internal development of Scottish society in accordance with "universal laws" simply could not explain the archaeological data from Scotland; reference to Continental data actually documented the solvent effects of external factors' (1958a, 73). Here it is noteworthy that in the previous year he had made it clear that he saw the Soviet approach to be a reaction against the ideology of imperialism rather than an understanding of the work of Marx or Engels.

> I cannot altogether avoid the feeling that Soviet prehistorians have gone further than necessary in their revulsion from German theory. Their rejection of prehistoric migration is not inspired by any text in Marx and Engels known to me, but is I suspect an addition to the Materialist Conception of History prompted by the special conditions of international politics, a counter blast to ideological imperialism. (1945d, 6)

Indeed it is clear that Childe's thinking was never in keeping with the Soviet orthodox view. In the context of his historical and philosophical theory he was seen to deviate from the latter in two important ways. First he did not employ the dialectical laws current in Soviet theory and secondly he gave little emphasis to the role of class in the historical process.

In the U.S.S.R. the laws of the dialectic had been elevated to the status of ultimate laws of nature from which all others are derived (Jordan 1967, 394f.). Marx's approach to history and society was thus seen as subordinate to the laws of the dialectic on which it was considered to have been based and from which it gained its meaning. In effect, then, the laws of the dialectic were raised above the historical process representing eternal laws immune from change. Obviously they could find no place in Childe's view of reality which denied transcendence of any kind, either religious or non-religious.

In his discussion of Marxism in *History* (1947), Childe omitted to deal with the laws of the dialectic or to acknowledge their increased importance in Soviet theory. Indeed it can be argued that it was only through this omission that he was able to represent 'dialectical materialism' as 'a view of history freed from transcendentalism and dependence on external laws' (1947b, 68). In *History*, then, Childe chose to represent Marxism as a principle of historical analysis rather than as a vision of the laws of change operating on all levels of phenomena. Nevertheless by refusing to openly criticise the dialectical laws it would seem that he was reluctant to express the very basic differences between his view of Marxism and that propagated in the U.S.S.R. at that time.

What Childe could not avoid, however, was a rather unorthodox attitude towards other crucial aspects of Marxist theory. This is particularly true of his approach to the problem of prediction. Unlike the Soviet Marxists Childe did not consider a stage of world communism to be the necessary outcome of the historical process according to the laws of dialectical materialism.

> It is doubtless a fitting goal, but not one to which history leads fatally and inevitably. There is no guarantee that our society will not vanish like the Mayan or become fossilized like the Chinese, no guarantee that *Homo Sapiens* will not become as extinct as Archaeopterix or Hipparion.
> (1947b, 81)

Childe's refusal to acknowledge the existence of the dialectical laws can be taken as an implicit rejection of their validity and consequently of their role as predictive tools. Furthermore, there are hints that his faith in the progressive nature of the historical process was beginning to wane towards the end of his career. As noted previously it had been severely shaken by the Second World War when he became convinced that European civilisation was irrevocably heading for another Dark Age. By the early fifties it seems that this apprehension had grown since now he was no longer thinking in terms of the end of European civilisation but rather of impending 'cosmic catastrophe'. Nevertheless despite this underlying pessimism it is interesting that he still upheld Marxism as a possible means of salvation and the Marxist vision of communist society as a possible alternative to his own catastrophic prophecy.

> For thirty years of the prolonged death agony of bourgeois civilization in western Europe, the *Labour Monthly* has consistently exposed the ideological distortions in which real issues are obscured in social consciousness. Every month its masterly analyses of the internal and foreign economic, industrial and political situation have uncovered the substantial trends and presented its readers with grim realities. But it has just as consistently been able to point out rational routes that from time to time might have avoided disaster. For its analyses have been constantly illumined by the positive vision of a classless and peace-

able society as the logical culmination of the historical process. Today, as cosmic catastrophe looms daily nearer the stimulus of the *Labour Monthly* is still more needed. (1951c, 342)

The second major deviation from the Soviet norm concerned the use of the concept of class. As indicated in chapter 4 both Hill and Thomson considered his treatment of this concept to be unsatisfactory. While the former believed that he had underplayed the role of class conflict in the historical process, the latter argued that he had not given sufficient emphasis to the class basis of the various types of historical orders. These criticisms were in keeping with the current Soviet view of the importance of the relations of production vis-à-vis the means of production. While Childe had never denied the significance of the productive relations in the development of society he remained remarkably uninfluenced by his Marxist contemporaries' emphasis on class, but throughout his career remained true to his techno-economic interpretation of Marxism. Presumably it was this apparent disinterest in class which led Thomson to underestimate Childe's understanding of class in historical analyses. As noted above one of Childe's first priorities in *History* was to place the historian in a social class and to emphasise both his allegiance to that class and the influence of his class outlook on his view of the past.

However, despite these criticisms *History* was well received among Childe's fellow Marxists in Britain, who considered it 'to amount to a demonstration that historical materialism is the only satisfactory interpretation of history' (Lilley 1949, 263). With the publication of *History*, then, Childe not only made his commitment to a Marxist model explicit but allowed the reader to follow the intellectual path leading him to that point. Perhaps above all, however, *History* illustrated Childe's dispassionate search for a key to understanding the historical process. That this search led him to Marxism was perhaps inevitable in view of his understanding of reality. That it diverged considerably from the orthodox was perhaps also inevitable on account of Childe's intellectual sincerity – clearly it was not his purpose to validate the official Russian viewpoint.

To say that Childe diverged from the Soviet viewpoint, however, is not to say that his approach is un-Marxist, for as Saville has noted, Marxism and Soviet scholarship are not necessarily one and the same. Indeed he has argued that it is the mistaken identification between them which has damaged the reputation of Marxist studies.

> Since Soviet writings in the fields of history and the social sciences, with few exceptions, has been at best uninteresting and at worst a farrago of quotation mongering dogmatism and biased selection, the consequences for the reputation of Marxist studies have been depressing.
> (Saville 1975, 5)

During Childe's lifetime British archaeologists on the whole were largely unacquainted with the principles of Marxism, seeing it primarily as political dogma rather than a historical model (Daniel 1949, 1958). Even today it is often represented as a crude mechanistic materialism (Clark 1976)

Until recently it seemed that Childe was quite content to leave his colleagues in ignorance both of the fundamentals of the Marxist approach and its relevance to prehistory – his comprehensive writings were for the most part outside a specifically archaeological context, either in theoretical texts such as *History* or radical journals such as *The Modern Quarterly*. The brief allusions to Marxism in popular works such as *Man Makes Himself* or *What Happened in History*, or to Marrism in *Scotland Before the Scots* were hardly conducive to an appreciation of the complexities or subtleties of historical materialism.

However, on one occasion Childe did attempt to explain in some detail the basic premises of Marxism and to demonstrate its usefulness as an interpretative tool for archaeologists. The article 'Prehistory and Marxism' was written in response to a paper by Daniel in the *Cambridge Journal* (1949) in which the propagandist nature of Soviet prehistory was strongly criticised. Thirty years after it was written 'Prehistory and Marxism' has finally been published in *Antiquity* (1979) (at the time Michael Oakshott, the editor of the *Cambridge Journal*, could not find room to publish). Here as in *History* Childe was concerned to emphasise that Marxist determinism was not mechanistic.

> It is deterministic in as much as it assumes that the historical process is not a mere succession of inexplicable or miraculous happenings, but that all the constituent events are interrelated and form an intelligible pattern. But the relations are not conceived mechanistically. The process is not repetitive or predetermined as are the operations of a machine which, however complicated, grinds out just that

which it was built to make and nothing else. It produces a pattern none the less, and its uncompleted portions must harmonize with what is already there, though there may be various combinations to complete the pattern. (1979, 93)

Marxism was materialistic in Childe's eyes in that it took a basic biological fact that man must eat to live as the first clue to understanding the patterns in the historical process.

It starts from the obvious fact that men cannot live without eating. So a society cannot exist unless its members can secure enough food to keep alive and reproduce. In any society approved beliefs or institutions that cut off the food-supply altogether (if for instance all Egyptian peasants had felt obliged to work all year round building a superpyramid), or stopped reproduction (as an universal and fanatical conviction of the virtue of celibacy would do), the society in question would soon come to an end. In this limiting case it is quite obvious that the food supply must exercise a final control in determining even beliefs and ideals. Presumably then, methods of getting a living in the end exercise a similar control more concretely. The way people get their living should be expected in the long run to 'determine' their beliefs and institutions. (1979, 93)

Childe sharply differentiated Marxism from environmentalism or geographical determinism by its emphasis on the interplay between technology, society and the environment, and by its focus on society rather than the individual.

As regards the classification of society, he pointed out that the Morgan–Engels model could only be used on a general level. Within each of the three stages there would be a wide range of economic systems and thus a corresponding variety of social and ideological superstructures. Marxists then, according to Childe, were more cautious than other prehistorians in their use of ethnographic parallels.

While Childe diverged from Soviet orthodoxy, he was not unsympathetic towards Soviet policy or scholarship. Indeed, on the contrary, throughout his career he spoke favourably both of the experiment in socialism in the U.S.S.R. and of Soviet learning. In 1935 for example, in reviewing his visit to the U.S.S.R. in the previous year for the Prehistoric Society, he expressed his approval of the co-ordination of archaeological research under the State Academy of the History of Material Culture (G.A.I.M.K.) in Leningrad, openly praising the organisation of the new state museums (1935d). Although he was not unaware of the propagandist nature of Soviet archaeology, his report underplayed the degree of state control over the archaeologist's thinking, making no reference to the disappearance of dissident archaeologists. It was hardly surprising then that his article provoked a reply stressing just these points. In 'Russian Archaeology: the other side of the picture' (1936) Clark thus attempted to balance Childe's rather rosy description of Russian archaeology. Drawing on Professor Tallgreen's account of Soviet prehistory, he conceded that the museum organisation might merit some praise. But he emphasised that this had been totally enforced by the state and that it had coincided with the disappearance of many notable Russian archaeologists.

> The fact we wish to underline is that the re-arrangement of museum collections has been carried out in accordance with 'new *obligatory* rules'. Archaeology in Russia has, in fact, become a department of Bolshevik propaganda. It is, moreover, clear from Professor Tallgreen's account that savants who have declined to submit to the dictation of the propaganda chiefs have been ruthlessly removed.
> (Clark 1936, 248)

Childe did not reply directly to Clark's article, but in 1940 in another report on Soviet archaeology he expressed concern 'lest dislike of the Soviet's foreign or domestic policy should lead men of science to take an unduly gloomy view of the position of archaeology in Russia' (1940b, 110). Here he attempted to draw attention to improvements in Russian archaeology since his visit in 1934, referring to new publications, in particular *Sovietskaya Archaeologiya*, which he argued was better than the earlier journals. Nevertheless he had to admit that the sentiments expressed in the editorial were discouraging, in particular the following view of Soviet archaeology.

> La Lutte implacable contre les écrits pseudo-scientifiques fascistes en matière d'archéologie, le dévoilement incessant des falsifications fascistes des faits archéologiques constituent le devoir direct des archéologues soviétiques qui édifient la véritable science objective; La Lutte sans merci contre les altérations de tout genre du marxisme-léninisme. (1940b, 110)

Interestingly, however, he did on this occasion attempt to defend the Russian sociological model of prehistory.

'Gentile', 'pre-class' . . . may be inconvenient categories. I doubt if they are really more deceptive than the terms 'neolithic', 'Bronze Age' as used in English as late as ten years ago. Prehistoric archaeology, being based so largely on a study of tools and weapons naturally lends itself to a 'materialist' interpretation. (1940b, 110)

In 1952 in 'Archaeological Organization in the u.s.s.r.' Childe wrote another staunch defence of Russian archaeology, comparing it favourably with its British counterpart. As early as 1940 he had argued that in Britain not only was the scientific status of the discipline unrecognised but the government did not give it enough financial aid. As a result archaeologists were forced to compete with each other for limited financial resources, this in turn having a detrimental effect on their work, since it led to an emphasis on sites of special interest rather than the less attractive, though no less theoretically important, domestic sites. In the Soviet Union, however, because archaeology was totally integrated within the state system, archaeologists could concentrate on the total excavation of domestic sites in order to obtain knowledge about rural economy, population density, social structure, etc. Furthermore, sites could be selected in order to solve theoretical problems. Unlike the British archaeologists, the Soviets were not distracted by the need to select sites 'likely to yield show pieces for display in museum cases nor buildings that can be opened to the public at 6d per head' (1952d, 25)

Similarly, he defended the freedom of thought in the u.s.s.r. arguing that Marxism as a philosophy of history did not restrict the archaeologist's approach.

> Let me remind you that Marxism does not mean a set of dogmas as to what happened in the past (such would save you the trouble of excavating to find out) but a method of interpretation and a system of values. (1952d, 25)

As regards publication he attempted rather unconvincingly to argue that the British archaeologist was in fact as restricted as his Soviet counterpart, since both were competing with their colleagues for the limited space available in archaeological journals. What he omitted to refer to, however, was the degree of censorship prevalent in the u.s.s.r.

Here it should be noted that Childe's article is of special interest in that it was written shortly after Stalin's denunciation of Marr in *Pravda* (1950). As indicated above the latter had exerted a profound influence on the course of Soviet archaeology since the revolution, and had been largely responsible for the narrow evolutionist view of socio-cultural change adopted by the party. According to this viewpoint cultural development was seen solely as an auchthonomous and stage-by-stage process, i.e. as a pattern of parallel evolution. His denunciation by Stalin thus marked a significant turning point in Soviet archaeology, opening the way for the acceptance of diffusion and migration as explanations of culture change.

From his article it is clear that Childe positively welcomed the change in direction, for he had never approved of the Soviet rejection of diffusion and migration as explanatory concepts. Indeed as noted previously he saw this primarily as a reaction against western theory – here, he terms it 'an ideological defence against Hitlerism' (1952d, 26)

Four years later in *Piecing Together the Past* (1956) Childe argued that the rejection of diffusion in the Soviet Union prior to 1950 was not without beneficial results for the study of prehistory.

> This sort of approach in fact obliges the prehistorian to undertake a much profounder study of the cultures concerned than is demanded for facile migrationist interpretations and so leads to a deeper appreciation of neglected aspects of the data. (1956a, 153)

At the same time, however, he was critical of the mechanistic interpretation of Marx propagated in the Soviet Union during this period.

> Karl Marx . . . argued quite convincingly that means of production and relations of production are inter-dependent in the sense that a technology can only function within an appropriate economy or system for distributing the product and that the relations of production in turn determine in the long run the ideological superstructure – codes of morality and law, superstitions, religious beliefs, artistic expression and so on. Briefly this is equivalent to saying that what we have called material culture determines spiritual culture. Many Marxists, even in Russia before 1950, confused 'determines' with 'causes'. . . .
> In fact of course the determination by technology Marx postulated was anything but mechanical causation. (1956a, 53)

In 'Valediction', his final address to students and staff at the

Institute of Archaeology in London, Childe again took the opportunity to denounce the Marrist phase of Soviet pre-history.

> Universal laws of social development are far fewer and far less reliable than Marrists before 1950 thought. . . . The Marrists' appeal to 'uniformities of social evolution' while it seemed to make intelligible the development of each individual culture to which they applied it, completely failed to explain the differences between one culture and another and indeed obliterated or dismissed as irrelevant differences observed. (1958c, 5–7)

There is no need, however, to see this as a rejection of Marxist theory as a whole (Clark 1976, 3, 9), but rather of its misinterpretation in the Soviet Union by Marrist archaeologists. Certainly it was no new stance and cannot be interpreted as a final disillusionment with historical materialism.

As a result of his unorthodox approach Childe's work was never wholly accepted in Russia.

> Among bourgeois scholars, there are not only our ideological enemies there are also progressive scholars who are friends of our country and who understand very well the universal significance of our science. One of these persons among English archaeologists for example, is Gordon Childe. Childe has not yet succeeded in overcoming many of the errors of bourgeois science. But he understands that scientific truth is in the socialist camp and is not ashamed to call himself a pupil of Soviet archaeologists.
> (Mongait (1950) in Miller 1956, 151)

While Childe's journey into Marxism led him into the realms of Soviet scholarship, his course was relatively unaltered by contact with the latter. Thus the Marxism of Childe was always an individual interpretation on Childe's part. Childe never adhered to popular or orthodox conceptions but took from Marx what would best serve his archaeological purpose. For Childe, Marxism could serve archaeology, he did not try to subserve the discipline to a political, to an 'outsider' philosophy.

Childe was never content to remain within the confines of any particular theoretical system be it Marxism, diffusionism or functionalism. Rather he attempted to synthetise these systems in order to achieve a comprehensive approach to prehistory which would apply to all levels of socio-cultural phenomena, and at the same time would offer him a model of socio-cultural change. For Childe there was a pattern to prehistory beyond the succession of events in time, and it was towards discovering and explaining that pattern that he devoted his lifework.

Select Bibliography

ABBREVIATIONS

A.J.A. = American Journal of Archaeology
B.S.A. = Annual of the British School of Athens
J.H.S. = Journal of the Hellenic Society
J.R.A.I. = Journal of the
Royal Anthropological Institute
P.P.S. = Proceedings of the Prehistoric Society
P.S.A.S. = Proceedings of the Society of Antiquaries
of Scotland

Acton, H. B. (1974) 'The Marxist Outlook', *Philosophy 22*,
208–30.
— (1955) *The Illusion of the Epoch: Marxism-Leninism as a
Philosophical Creed*. London.
Adams, R. McC. (1966) *The Evolution of Urban Society*.
Chicago.
— (1968) 'Archaeological Research Strategies, Past and
Present', *Science CLX*, 118–92.
Allen, J. (1967) 'Aspects of V. Gordon Childe', *Labour and
History XII*, 52–9.
Bagby, P. H.(1953) 'Culture and the Causes of Culture',
American Anthropologist 55, 535–54.
Banton, M. P. (Ed.) (1961) *Darwinism and the Study of
Society*. London.
Barker, E., Clark, G., and Vaucher, P. (Eds) (1954) *The
European Inheritance*. Oxford.
Bierstedt, R. (1966) *Emile Durkheim*. London.
Binford, L. R. (1968) 'Archaeological Perspectives' in
(Binford, S. R. and Binford, L. R. (Eds) 1968) 5–32.
— (1968) 'Post Pleistocene Adaptations' in (Binford, S. R.
and Binford, L. R. (Eds) 1968) 313–41.
— (1972a) 'Archaeology as Anthropology' in (Leone, M.
(Ed.) 1972) 93–101.

— (1972b) 'Archaeological Systematics and the Study of
    Culture Process' in (Leone, M. (Ed.)) 125–32.

Binford, S. R. and Binford, L. R. (Eds) (1968) *New
    Perspectives in Archaeology*. Chicago.

Birdsell, J. (1958) 'On Population Structure in Generalised
    Hunting and Collecting Populations', *Evolution 12 (2)*
    189–205.

— (1968) 'Some Predictions for the Pleistocene Based on
    Equilibrium Systems among Recent Hunter Gatherers' in
    (Lee, R. B. and De Vore, I. (Eds)) 229–40.

Bloch, M. (1975) *Marxist Analyses and Social Anthropology*.
    London.

Bober, M. (1927) *Karl Marx's Interpretation of History*.
    Cambridge (Mass.).

Boserup, E. (1965) *The Conditions of Agricultural Growth:
    The Economics of Agrarian Change under Population
    Pressure*. London.

Bottomore, T. B. (1956) *Marx's Social Theory*. London.

— (1963) *Introduction to Karl Marx*. London.

Bottomore, T. B. and Rubel, M. (Eds) (1956) *Karl Marx:
    Selected Writings in Sociology and Social Philosophy*.
    London.

Braidwood, R. J. (1951) *Prehistoric Men*. Chicago.

— (1952) 'From Cave to Village', *Scientific American
    187 (4)* 62–6.

— (1960) 'The Agricultural Revolution', *Scientific American
    203*, 130–41.

— (1960) 'Levels in Prehistory: a model for consideration of
    the evidence' in (Tax, S. (Ed.) 1960) (2), 143–52.

Braidwood, R. J. and Howe, B. (1960) *Prehistoric
    Investigations in Iraqi Kurdistan*. Chicago.

Braidwood, R. J. and Willey, G. R. (Eds) (1962) *Courses
    Towards Urban Life*. Edinburgh.

Braithwaite, R. B. (1960) *Scientific Explanation*. New York.

Bray, W. (1973) 'The Biological Basis of Culture' in (Renfrew,
    C. (Ed.) 1973) 73–92.

Brown, J. A. (1892) 'On the Continuity of the Palaeolithic to
    Neolithic Period', *J.R.A.I. 22*, 69–98.

Burkitt, M. C. (1923) *Our Forerunners*. London.

Burnham, P. (1973) 'The Explanatory Value of the Concept of
    Adaptation in Studies of Culture Change' in (Renfrew, C.
    (Ed.) 1973) 93–104.

Bury, H.J. (1932) *The Idea of Progress*. New York.

Chang, K.C. (1967) *Rethinking Archaeology*. New York.

Childe, V.G. (1915) 'On the Date and Origin of Minyan Ware', *J.H.S. XXXV*, 196–207.

— (1922) 'The Present State of Archaeological Studies in Central Europe', *Man xxii*, No. 69.

— (1923a) *How Labour Governs*. London.

— (1923b) 'Obituary: Jaroslav Palliardi', *Man xxiii*, No. 64.

— (1925a) *The Dawn of European Civilization*. London.

— (1925b) 'Obituary: Dr. Ferencz Laszlo', *Man xxv* no.110.

— (1925c) 'When Did the Beaker Folk Arrive?', *Archaeologia LXIV*, 159–78.

— (1926a) *The Aryans*. London.

— (1926b) 'Traces of the Aryans on the Middle Danube', *Man xxv*, No. 100.

— (1927a) *The Dawn of European Civilization* (2nd edition). London.

— (1927b) 'The Danube Thoroughfare and the Beginnings of Civilization in Europe', *Antiquity I*, 79–91.

— (1928) *The Most Ancient East: the Oriental Prelude to European Prehistory*. London.

— (1929) *The Danube in Prehistory*. Oxford.

— (1930a) *The Bronze Age*. Cambridge.

— (1930b) 'New Views on the Relations of the Aegean and the North Balkans', *J.H.S. 50 (2)*, 255–62.

— (1931a) *Skara Brae: A Pictish Village in Orkney*. London.

— (1931b) 'The Forest Cultures of Northern Europe: A study in Evolution and Diffusion', *J.R.A.I. LXI*, 325–48.

— (1932a) 'A Chronological Table of Prehistory' (with M.C. Burkitt), *Antiquity VI*, 185–205.

— (1932b) 'Russia: a new anthropological museum', *Man xxxii*, No. 53.

— (1933a) 'Is Prehistory Practical?' *Antiquity VII*, 410–18.

— (1933b) 'Races, Peoples and Cultures in Prehistoric Europe', *History* N.S. *XVIII*, No. 21, 193–203.

— (1934) *New Light on the Most Ancient East, the Oriental prelude to European prehistory*. London.

— (1935a) *New Light on the Most Ancient East* (2nd Edition, revised). London.

— (1935b) *The Prehistory of Scotland*. London.

— (1935c) 'Changing Methods and Aims in Prehistory: Presidential Address for 1935', *P.P.S. I*, 1–15.

Childe, V. G. (1935d) 'Prehistory in the U.S.S.R.', *P.P.S. I*, 151–4.

— (1936a) *Man Makes Himself*. London.

— (1936b) 'The Antiquity of Nordic Culture', *Man xxxvi*, No. 83.

— (1936c) 'International Congresses on the Science of Man', *Nature 137*, 1074.

— (1936d) 'Man and Forest in Prehistoric Europe' (review of *The Mesolithic Settlement of Northern Europe* by J. C. D. Clark), *Nature 138*, 95.

— (1937a) 'Neolithic Black Ware in Greece and on the Danube', *B.S.A. xxxvii*, 26–35.

— (1937b) 'Adaptation to the Post Glacial Forest on the North Eurasiatic Plain', in (MacCurdy, C. J. (Ed.) 1937) 233–42.

— (1937c) 'A Prehistorian's Interpretation of Diffusion', in (Harvard Tercentenary Publications (Ed.) 1937) 3–21.

— (1937d) 'The Antiquity of the British Bronze Age', *American Anthropologist 39*, 1–22.

— (1937e) 'The Indus Civilization', *Antiquity XI*, 351.

— (1938) 'The Orient and Europe: Presidential Address to Section H (Anthropology) of the British Association', The Advancement of Science 1938, 181–96.

— (1939a) *The Dawn of European Civilization* (3rd edition, revised and reset). London.

— (1939b) 'The Orient and Europe', *A.J.A. XLIV*, 10–26.

— (1940a) *Prehistoric Communities of the British Isles*. London and Edinburgh.

— (1940b) 'Archaeology in the U.S.S.R.', *Nature 145*, 110–11.

— (1941) 'The History of Civilization', *Antiquity XV*, 1–14.

— (1942a) *What Happened in History*. Harmondsworth.

— (1942b) 'Prehistory in the U.S.S.R. I. Palaeolithic and Mesolithic. A. Caucasus and Crimea', *Man xlii*, No. 59.

— (1942c) 'Prehistory in the U.S.S.R. I. Palaeolithic and Mesolithic. B. The Russian Plain', *Man xlii*, No. 60.

— (1942d) 'Prehistory in the U.S.S.R. II. The Copper Age in South Russia', *Man xlii*, No. 74.

— (1943a) 'The Study of Anthropology', *Antiquity XVII*, 213–14.

— (1943b) 'Archaeology in the U.S.S.R. The Forest Zone', *Man xliii*, No. 2.

Childe, V. G. (1943c) 'The Mesolithic and Neolithic in Northern Europe', *Man xliii*, No. 17.

— (1943d) 'Archaeology as a Science', *Nature 152*, 22–3.

— (1944a) *The Story of Tools*. London.

— (1944b) 'Archaeological Ages as Technological Stages: Huxley Memorial Lecture, 1944', *J.R.A.I. LXXIV*, 7–24.

— (1944c) 'The Future of Archaeology', *Man xliv*, No. 7.

— (1944d) 'Recent Excavations on Prehistoric Sites in Soviet Russia', *Man xliv*, No. 29.

— (1944e) 'Historical Analysis of Archaeological Method' (Review of *The Three Ages* by G. E. Daniel), *Nature 153*, 206–7.

— (1945a) *Progress and Archaeology*. London.

— (1945b) 'Archaeology and Anthropology in the U.S.S.R.', *Nature 156*, 224–5.

— (1945c) 'Rational Order in History', *The Rationalist Annual*, 1945, 21–6.

— (1945d) 'Introduction to the Conference on the Problems and Prospects of European Archaeology' (16–17 September 1944), *University of London Institute of Archaeology, Occasional Paper*, No. 6, 6–12.

— (1946a) *Scotland Before the Scots*: being the Rhind Lectures for 1944. London.

— (1946b) 'Human Cultures as Adaptations to Environment', *Geog. Journal CVIII*, Nos. 4–6, 227–30.

— (1946c) 'The Social Implications of the Three "Ages" in Archaeological Classification', *The Modern Quarterly*, N.S.*I.*, 18–33.

— (1946d) 'Archaeology and Anthropology', *Southwestern Journal of Anthropology 2*, No. 3, 243–51.

— (1947a) *The Dawn of European Civilization* (4th edition, revised and reset). London.

— (1947b) *History*. London.

— (1947c) 'The Final Bronze Age in the Near East and in Temperate Europe', *Arch. News Letter 2*, 9–11.

— (1947d) *Archaeology as a Social Science*: Inaugural Lecture. University of London, Institute of Archaeology, Third Annual Report, 49–60.

— (1948) 'Culture Sequence in the Stone Age of Northern Europe', *Man xlviii*, No. 44.

Childe, V. G. (1949a) *Social Worlds of Knowledge*. London. L. T. Hobhouse Memorial Trust Lecture, No. 19, delivered on 12 May 1948 at King's College, London.

— (1949b) 'The Origin of Neolithic Culture in Northern Europe', *Antiquity XXIII*, 129–35.

— (1949c) 'The Sociology of Knowledge', *The Modern Quarterly* N.S. *IV*, 302–9.

— (1949d) 'Organic and Social Evolution', *The Rationalist Annual*, 1949, 57–62.

— (1950a) *The Dawn of European Civilization* (5th edition, revised). London.

— (1950b) *Prehistoric Migrations in Europe*. London.

— (1950c) *Magic Craftsmanship and Science*. The Frazer Lecture, delivered at Liverpool on 10 November 1949. Liverpool.

— (1950d) 'Social Evolution in the Light of Archaeology', *Mankind 4* No. 5, 175–83.

— (1950e) 'The Urban Revolution', *The Town Planning Review XXI*, No. 1, 3–17.

— (1951a) *Social Evolution*. London.

— (1951b) 'The Framework of Prehistory', *Man li*, No. 119.

— (1951c) '30th Anniversary Messages of Greeting', *Labour Monthly 33*, No. 7, 342.

— (1952a) *New Light on the Most Ancient East* (4th edition, rewritten). London.

— (1952b) *Old World Neolithic*. Inventory Paper for the Wenner-Gren International Symposium on Anthropology. New York City, 9–20 June 1952; Paper No. 10, 1–21, duplicated.

— (1952c) 'The Birth of Civilization', *Past and Present 2*, 1–10.

— (1952d) 'Archaeological Organization in the U.S.S.R.', *The Anglo-Soviet Journal 13 (3)*, 23–6.

— (1953) 'The Constitution of Archaeology as a Science', in (Underwood, E. A. (Ed.) 1953) 3–15.

— (1954a) 'Prehistory. 1. Man and His Culture. 2. Pleistocene Societies in Europe. 3. The Mesolithic Age', in (Barker, E., Clark, G. and Vaucher, P. (Eds.) 1954) 11–27, 29–38.

— (1954b) 'Early Forms of Society' in (Singer, C., Holmyard, E. J., and Hall, A. R. (Eds.) 1954) 38–57.

Childe, V.G. (1954c) 'The Stone Age Comes to Life', *The Rationalist Annual* 1954, 1–7.
— (1956a) *Piecing Together the Past: The Interpretation of Archaeological Data*. London.
— (1956b) *A Short Introduction to Archaeology*. London.
— (1956c) *Society and Knowledge*. New York.
— (1956d) 'The Past, The Present and The Future' (Review of History in a Changing World by G. Barraclough), *Past and Present 10*, 3–5.
— (1957a) *The Dawn of European Civilization* (6th edition, revised). London.
— (1957b) 'The Bronze Age', *Past and Present 12*, 2–15.
— (1958a) 'Retrospect', *Antiquity 32*, 69–74.
— (1958b) *The Prehistory of European Society*. Harmondsworth.
— (1958c) 'Valediction', *Bull. Inst. Archaeol. London Univ.*, 1, 1–8.
— (1979) 'Prehistory and Marxism', *Antiquity LIII*, 93–7.
Clark, J.G.D. (1936) 'Russian Archaeology: the other side of the Picture', *P.P.S. 2*, 248–9.
— (1952) *Prehistoric Europe: the Economic Basis*. London.
— (1965) 'Radiocarbon Dating and the Expansion of Farming Culture from the Near East over Europe', *P.P.S. XXXI*, 58–73.
— (1966) 'The Invasion Hypothesis in British Archaeology', *Antiquity 40*, 172–9.
— (1976) 'Prehistory since Childe', *Bull. Inst. Archaeol. London Univ.*
Clarke, D. (1968) *Analytical Archaeology*. London.
— (Ed.) (1972) *Models in Archaeology*. London.
— (1973) 'Archaeology: the loss of Innocence', *Antiquity 47*, 6–18.
Clauson, G. (Sir) (1973) 'Philology and Archaeology', *Antiquity XLVII*, 37–43.
Cole, G. (1934) *What Marx Really Meant*. London and Southampton.
Collins, D. (1973) 'Epistemology and Culture Tradition Theory' in (Renfrew, C. (Ed.) 1973) 53–8.
Collingwood, R.G. (1946) *The Idea of History*. Oxford.
Cornforth, M. (1952) *Dialectical Materialism: an Introductory Course*. London.
— (1965) *Marxism and the Linguistic Philosophy*. London.

Crawford, O. G. S. (1921) *Man and His Past*. Oxford.
— (1926) Review of The Dawn of European Civilization by
  V. Gordon Childe, *Antiquaries Journal 6*, 89–90.
— (1936) 'Human Progress; a review' (of *Man Makes
  Himself* by V. Gordon Childe), *Antiquity 10*, 391–404.
— (1943) Review of What Happened in History by
  V. Gordon Childe, *Antiquity 17*, 101–3.
Daniel, G. (1943) *The Three Ages*. Cambridge.
— (1949) 'A Defence of Prehistory', *The Cambridge Journal
  3*, 131–47.
— (1950) *A Hundred Years of Archaeology*. London.
— (1958) Editorial, *Antiquity 32*, 65–8.
— (1962) *The Idea of Prehistory*. London.
— (1967) *The Origins and Growth of Archaeology*.
  Harmondsworth.
— (1968) *The First Civilizations: The Archaeology of their
  Origins*. London.
— (1971) 'From Worsaae to Childe: the models of
  prehistory', *P.P.S. 38*, 34–9.
— (1975) *A Hundred and Fifty Years of Archaeology*.
  London.
— (1977) Editorial, *Antiquity LI*, 3, 4.
Darlington, C. D. (1969) *The Evolution of Man and Society*.
  London.
Darwin, C. (1875) *The Variation of Plants and Animals under
  Domestication*. London.
Dawkins, W. B. (1894) 'On the Relation of the Palaeolithic to
  the Neolithic Period', *J.R.A.I. 23*, 242–54.
Deevy, E. S. (1960) 'The Human Population', *Scientific
  American 203*, 1, 194–204.
de Pradenne, V. (1935) 'The World Wide Expansion of
  Culture', *Antiquity IX*, 305–10.
Dobb, M. (1966) 'Marx on Pre-Capitalist Economic
  Formations', *Science and Society 30*, 319–25.
Dumond, D. E. (1965) 'Population Growth and Cultural
  Change', *Southwestern Journal of Anthropology 21*, 4,
  302–24.
Durkheim, E. (1915) *The Elementary Forms of Religious Life*
  (trans. J. W. Swain). London and New York.
Dutt, R. P. (1957) 'Professor V. Gordon Childe', *The Times*,
  Oct. 24. London.

Ellis, J. and Davies, R. W. (1951) 'The Crisis in Soviet Linguistics', *Soviet Studies 2*, 209–65.

Engels, F. (1935) *Anti-Duhring* (trans. E. Burns). London. (Orig. 1878.)

— (1940) *Dialectics of Nature* (trans. E. Burns) London. (Orig. 1876.)

— (1940) *The Origin of the Family Private Property and the State* (trans. A. West). London. (Orig. 1884.)

Firth, R. (1975) 'The Sceptical Anthropologist? Social Anthropology and Marxist Views on Society' in (Bloch, M. (Ed.) 1975), 29–60.

Flannery, K. V. (1968) 'Origins and Ecological Effects of Early Domestication in Iran and the Near East' in (Ucko, P. J. and Dimbleby, G. W. (Eds.) 1968) 73–100.

Ford, J. A. (1954) 'The Type Concept Revisited', *American Anthropologist 56(1)*, 42–54.

Friedman, J. and Rowlands, M. J. (1978) *The Evolution of Social Systems*. London.

Fritz, J. M. and Plog, F. (1970) 'The Nature of Archaeological Explanation', *American Antiquity 35*, 405–12.

Garn, S. (1957) 'Race and Evolution', *American Anthropologist 59*, 218–24.

Gathercole, P. (1971) 'Patterns in Prehistory: an Examination of the Later Thinking of V. Gordon Childe', *World Archaeology 3*, 225–32.

Goldenweiser, A. (1937) *Anthropology: An Introduction to Primitive Culture*. New York and London.

Gollan, R. (1964) Review of *How Labour Governs* by V. Gordon Childe, *Labour History 7*, 61–2.

Green, S. (1976) *A Biography of V. Gordon Childe* (unpublished BA thesis).

Greene, J. C. (1961) *Darwin and the Modern World View*. Houston, Texas.

Halbawchs, M. (1960) *Population and Society: An Introduction to Social Morphology*. Illinois.

Harlan, J. R. (1967) 'A Wild Wheat Harvest in Turkey', *Archaeology 20 (3)*, 197–201.

Harris, J. C. (1971) 'Explanation in Prehistory', *P.P.S. 37*, 38–55.

Harris, M. (1968) *The Rise of Anthropological Theory*. London.

Harvard Tercentenary Publications (1937) *Independence, Convergence and Borrowing in Institutions, Thought and Art*. Cambridge (Mass.).

Harvey, D. (1969) *Explanation in Geography*.

Hawkes, C. (1940) *The Prehistoric Foundations of Europe*. London.

— (1954) 'Archaeological Theory and Method: Some Suggestions from the Old World', *American Anthropologist 56 (1)*, 155–68.

— (1973) 'Innocence Retrieval in Archaeology', *Antiquity XLVII*, 176–9.

Heizer, R. F. (1962) 'The Background of Thomsen's Three Age System', *Technology and Culture 3*, 259–66.

Hempel, C. G. (1967) *Aspects of Scientific Explanation and Other Essays in the Philosophies of Science*. New York.

Hill, C. (1949) Review of History by V. Gordon Childe, *The Modern Quarterly* N.S. *4*, 259–62.

Hill, J. N. (1972) 'The Methodological Debate in Archaeology', in (Clarke, D. L. (Ed.) 1972) 61–108.

Hobsbawm, E. (Ed.) (1965) *Karl Marx: Introduction to Precapitalist Economic Formations*. New York.

Hodder, I. (Ed.) (1978) *The Spatial Organisation of Culture*. London.

Jordan, Z. (1967) *The Evolution of Dialectical Materialism: a Philosophical and Sociological Analysis*.

Klejn, L. S. (1970) 'Archaeology in Britain: A Marxist View', *Antiquity 44*, 296–303.

— (1973) 'Marxism, the Systemic Approach and Archaeology', in (Renfrew, C. (Ed.) 1973) 691–710.

Kossinna, G. (1911) *Die Herkunft der Germamen*. Leipzig.

— (1912) *Die Deutsche Vorgeschichte ein Hervorragend Nationale Wissenschaft*. Berlin.

— (1921) *Die Indogermanen*. Berlin.

Kroeber, A. (1952) *The Nature of Culture*. Chicago.

Kroeber, A. and Kluckholn (1952) *Culture, A Critical Review of Concepts and Definitions*. Cambridge (Mass.)

Leacock, S. (1963) Introduction to L. H. Morgan, *Ancient Society*, New York.

Lee, R. B. and de Vore, I. (Eds.) (1968) *Man the Hunter*. Chicago.

Leff, G. (1961) *The Tyranny of Concepts: A Critique of Marxism*. London.

Leone, M. (Ed.) (1972) *Contemporary Archaeology*.
Southern Illinois Univ. Press.

Lewis, C. and Short, C. (1966) *A Latin Dictionary*. Oxford.

Lilley, S. (1949) Review of *History* by V. Gordon Childe, *The
Modern Quarterly* N.S. *4*, 262–5.

Lowie, R. H. (1938) *The History of Ethnological Theory*.
London.

Lowther, G. R. (1962) 'Epistemology and Archaeological
Theory', *Current Anthropology III*, 195–509.

Lubbock, J. (1865) *Prehistoric Times, as Illustrated by Ancient
Remains and the Manners and Customs of Modern
Savages*. London.

Lukacs, G. (1966) 'Technology and Social Relations', *New
Left Review 39*, 27–30.

Lynch, B. P. and Lynch, T. F. (1968) 'The Beginnings of a
Scientific Approach to Prehistoric Archaeology in 17th
and 18th century Britain', *Southwestern Journal of
Anthropology 24*, 33–65.

MacAlister, R. (Ed.) (1921) *A Textbook of European
Archaeology*. Cambridge.

MacCurdy, C. G. (1937) *Early Man*. Philadelphia.

Malinowski, B. (1922) *Argonauts of the Western Pacific*.
New York.

— (1935) *Coral Gardens and their Magic*. London.

Mallory, J. P. 1976) 'Time Perspective and Proto Indo-
European Culture', *World Archaeology 8 (1)*, 44–56.

Mellar, D. H. (1973) 'Do Cultures Exist?', in (Renfrew, C.
(Ed.) 1973) 59–71.

Miller, M. (1951) 'Marr, Stalin and the Theory of Language',
Soviet Studies 2, 364–71.

— (1956) *Archaeology in the U.S.S.R.* New York.

Mongait, A. (1959) *Archaeology in the U.S.S.R.* Moscow.

Morgan, C. (1973) 'Archaeology and Explanation', *World
Archaeology 4*, 259–76.

Morgan, L. H. (1877) *Ancient Society*. New York.

Naroll, R. (1964) 'On Ethnic Unit Classification', *Current
Anthropology 5*, 283–91.

Oates, J. (1972) 'Prehistoric Settlement Patterns in
Mesopotamia', in (Ucko, J., Tringham, R. and
Dimbleby, G. W. (1972)) 299–310.

Ogden, C. and Richards, I. (1923) *The Meaning of Meaning*.
London and New York.

Peake, H. J. (1922) *The Bronze Age and Celtic World*. London.
— (1927) 'The Beginnings of Civilization', *J.R.A.I. 57*, 19–38.

Peake, H. J. and Fleure (1927) *The Corridors of Time*. Oxford.

Penniman, T. K. (1965) *A Hundred Years of Anthropology*. London.

Perry, W. J. (1923) *The Children of the Sun*. London.

Persons, S. (Ed.) (1950) *Evolutionary Thought in America*. New Haven.

Piggott, S. (1958a) 'The Dawn: And An Epilogue', *Antiquity 32*, 75–9.
— (1958b) 'Vere Gordon Childe', *Proc. Brit. Acad. XLIV*, 305–12.
— (1965) *Ancient Europe from the Beginnings of Agriculture to Classical Antiquity. A Survey*. Edinburgh.

Poliakov, L. (1974) *The Aryan Myth* (trans. E. Howard). London.

'Professor V. Gordon Childe: An Eminent Prehistorian' Obituary Notice. *The Times*, 21 Oct. 1957.

Radcliffe-Brown, A. R. (1935) 'On the Concept of Function in the Social Sciences', *American Anthropol. 37*, 394–402.
— (1952) *Structure and Function in Primitive Society*. London.

Ravetz, A. (1959) 'Notes on the Work of V. Gordon Childe', *New Reasoner 10*, 59–65.

Renfrew, C. (1967) 'Colonialism and Megalithismus', *Antiquity 41*, 276–88.
— (1969) 'Trade and Culture Process in Europe', *Current Anthropology 10*, 151–69.
— (1973) *Before Civilization: the radiocarbon revolution and prehistoric Europe*. London.
— (Ed.) (1973) *The Explanation of Culture Change: Models in Prehistory*. London.
— (1978) 'Space Time and Polity', in (Friedman and Rowlands (1978)) 89–112.
— (1979) *Problems in European Prehistory*. Edinburgh.

Rhind, A. H. (1856) 'On the History of the Systematic Classification of Primeval Relics', *Arch. Journal 13*, 209–14.

Rouse, I. (1965) 'The Place of Peoples in Prehistoric Research', *J.R.A.I. 95 (1)*, 1–15.

Saville, A. (1970) 'Towards a Past Pieced Together', *Bull. Univ. Birmingham Arch. Soc. 8 (2)*, 1–2.

Saville, J. (1974) *Marxism and History.* Hull.

Schaub, E. (1920) 'A Sociological Theory of Knowledge', *Philosophical Review 29,* 319–39.

Schmidt, A. (1971) *The Concept of Nature in Marx.* London.

Shennan, S. J. (1978) 'Archaeological Cultures, an Empirical Investigation', in (Hodder, I. (Ed.) 1978) 113–40.

Shinkin, D. B. (1949) 'Recent Trends in Soviet Archaeology', *American Anthropologist 51,* 621–5.

Singer, C., Holmyard, E. J. and Hall, A. R. (1954) *A History of Technology.* Oxford.

Slotkin, J. S. (1952) 'Some Basic Methodological Problems in Prehistory', *Southwestern Journal of Anthropology 8,* 442–3.

— (1965) *Readings in Early Anthropology.* New York.

Smith, Sir G. E. (1911) *The Ancient Egyptians and Their Influence Upon the Civilization of Europe.* London and New York.

— (1928) *In the Beginning: the Origin of Civilization.* London.

— (1933) *The Diffusion of Culture.* London.

Smith, I. F. (1955) 'Bibliography of the Publications of Professor V. Gordon Childe', *P.P.S. 21,* 295–304.

Smith, M. A. (1955) 'The Limitations of Inference in Archaeology', *The Arch. Newsletter 6 (1),* 1–7.

Smith, P. (1973) 'Changes in Population Pressure in Archaeological Explanation', *World Archaeology 4,* 5–18.

Snyder, L. (1939) *Race, a history of modern ethnic theories.* New York.

— (1962) *The Idea of Racialism.* Princeton.

Stalin, J. (1941) *Dialectical and Historical Materialism.* London.

Sterud, G. (1973) 'A Paradigmatic View of Prehistory', in (Renfrew, C. (Ed.) 1973) 3–18.

Tallgreen, A. M. (1937) 'The Method of Prehistoric Archaeology', *Antiquity 42,* 152–61.

Tax, S. (Ed.) (1960) *Evolution After Darwin* (3 vols.). Chicago.

Theodorson, G. A. and Theodorson, A. G. (1969) *A Modern Dictionary of Sociology.* London.

Thompson, M. W. (1965) 'Marxism and Culture', *Antiquity 39,* 108–13.

Thompson, R. (1956) 'The Subjective Element in
    Archaeological Inference', *Southwestern Journal of
    Anthropology 12 (3)*, 327–32.
Thomson, G. (1949) Review of *History* by V. Gordon Childe,
    The Modern Quarterly N.S. *4*, 260–3.
Tolstoy, P. (1952) 'Morgan and Soviet Anthropological
    Thought', *American Anthropologist 54*, 8–17.
Trigger, B. (1968a) 'Major Concepts of Archaeology in
    Historical Perspective', *Man 3*, 527–41.
— (1968b) *Beyond History : The Methods of Prehistory*. New
    York and London.
— (1970) 'Aims in Prehistoric Archaeology', *Antiquity 44*,
    26–37.
— (1978) *Time and Traditions*. Edinburgh.
Tringham, R. (1971) *Hunters, Fishers and Farmers of Eastern
    Europe*. London.
Tylor, E. (1871) *Primitive Culture*. London.
Ucko, P. and Dimbleby, G.W. (Eds.) (1969) *The
    Domestication and Exploitation of Plants and Animals*.
    London.
Ucko, P., Tringham, R. and Dimbleby, G.W. (Eds.) (1972)
    Man, Settlement and Urbanism. London.
Underwood, E.A. (Ed.) (1953) *Science, Medicine and
    History*. Essays on the Evolution of Scientific Thought and
    Medical Practice, written in Honour of Charles Singer.
Watson, R. (1972) 'The "New Archaeology" of the 1960s',
    Antiquity XLVI, 210–15.
Watson, R.J., Leblanc, S.A. and Redman, C.L. (1971)
    *Explanation in Archaeology: An Explicitly Scientific
    Approach*.
Westropp, H.M. (1872) *Prehistoric Phases; or Introductory
    Essays on Prehistoric Archaeology*. London.
Wheatley, P. (1972) 'The Concept of Urbanism', in (Ucko,
    Tringham and Dimbleby (Eds.) 1972) 601–37.
Wheeler, M. (1957) 'Professor V. Gordon Childe', *The Times*,
    Oct. 23rd. London.
Willey, G.R. and Sabloff, J.A. (1974) *A History of American
    Archaeology*. London.
Zohary, D. (1969) 'The progenitors of wheat and barley in
    relation to domestication and agricultural dispersal in the
    Old World', in (Ucko and Dimbleby (Eds.) 1969) 47–66.

Index